FROM GREAT TO PREEMINENT:

Success Tools for Overachievers

Vol. II

I0510501

This book is presented to:

Name:

_____

Presented by:

_____

Date:

_____

Comments:

FROM GREAT TO PREEMINENT:

Success Tools for Overachievers

Vol. II

<u>Contains the following lectures:</u>

Crossing the Threshold

Evolve Your Main Asset

The Workaholic

Never Satisfied

Bonus Lectures

*Strike a Nerve

*Stop Keeping Up With the Joneses

FROM GREAT TO PREEMINENT

Success Tools for Overachievers

Vol. II

by

E.M. ROBINSON, Ph.D.

Dr. E.M. Robinson & Associates, LLC.
© 2019
Grenada, MS

ISBN: 9781694011848

~ Your mind can only carry you so far; then you must work. ~

E.M. Robinson

-To Joshua, Elijah and Nadia with love.-

ACKNOWLEGEMENTS

This book is the result of more than forty years of counsel, training, research and experience throughout the course of my life.

The counselors to whom appreciation must be rendered begins with my father and mother. The entirety of my knowledge, resources, drive and intellect is, in some form, attributable to their unselfish pouring into me from birth.

The trainer of seminal value to whom many of the precepts explained in this book are based, is my late sibling, Eugene II. Through three plus decades, I learned and developed an understanding of business and risk that is continuously displayed through my actions and words.

I would be remiss in accounting for those who contributed to this book from the vantage point of research if I failed to cite my instructors at Mississippi Valley State University from 1994-1995 and 1997-2000. Albeit, too numerous to name specifically, I have been added to versus subtracted from due to their insistence to learn things thoroughly.

The last two individuals, who warrant praise for unselfishly offering their experiences to aid development of my knowledge, are James P. Hardiman, Jr. and Cedrick Edwards, MD. There will be no blade formed in this lifetime that is sharp enough to sever our ties.

In sum, my counselors, trainers, instructors and friends in business and education are the instruments through which my thinking has been shaped. I render to them all profuse thanks.

DEDICATION

This book is dedicated to two persons of character unmatched in my forty-two years of existence.

First, to my lifetime partner, Teneeshia: there is no person of equivalent value as we have become affixed in mind and soul for eternity.

Second, I must attest to the immeasurable worth of my sibling, Everett. Your adeptness in the production of sound is inferior to none.

NOTE TO READERS

This book serves as a means for the unselfish sharing of knowledge exhibited by innumerable instructors over the course of my lifetime. In this text, I posit some of the most valuable intellectual tools that have been to my boon in many areas of work. It is my sincerest hope that these ideas will permit you to accomplish anything that you conceive. In addition, please enjoy the bonus lectures which have been inserted to keep you progressing toward the achievement of your most compelling goals.

• NOTE •

Each lecture in this text is presented exactly as it is worded in audio form and retains expressions, terms and references that are applicable to audio only and not common to written communication.

CONTENTS

PREFACE

Are you just getting by or doing just enough to pass? If you are not making a difference and this state of mediocrity displeases you, this book is a necessity. As a matter of fact, this book is required.

This book is about you possessing a tremendous amount of talent but limiting yourself to the use of only one or a few of your skills. It's about you tilling the soil, but never planting, let alone reaping. It covers you squandering opportunities and allowing dust to settle on your big plans due to inaction. It deals with your failure to take the steps necessary to become addicted to the success that will foster increasingly higher levels of achievement. It even opens your eyes to you taking unnecessary shortcuts and encourages you to self-correct. This self-correction is a counteraction that will help you exhibit the fortitude to cross threshold after threshold on the journey to your goal.

For people who view themselves as underperformers, this text provides a rubric for overcoming years of inattention to the details of success. It accomplishes this by slicing success into pieces that can be easily inspected. From this close look at success, you become aware of the resources readily available to you. You also discover strength of mind, repercussions of inaction and motivators for achievement.

This deconstruction of success ensures that you comprehend the most contemporary definition of success as it has shifted from wealth and fame to happiness. In other words, this text helps you to clearly see personal satisfaction, a coveted virtue, as the result of a lifetime of employing proven tools for success. This highly sought outcome follows numerous steps taken in pursuit of the acquisition of wealth, vertical moves made on the organizational structure in which one works or the accomplishment of a goal that has required years of study, time and effort. But, more importantly and equivalent to the tools provided in Volume I of this series, this analysis assists you in creating a life of your own choosing by helping you to overcome recurring fear, doubt and procrastination.

Ukrainian pathophysiologist and author of the *Prolongation of Life*, Alexander A. Bogomolets, explains that one must not lose desires as they are mighty stimulants to creativeness, to love, and to a long life.[1] This statement is not only true, but a core rudiment of this text. Your desires are your motivators. They compel you seek to satisfy your psyche daily. They trigger the release of positive neurotransmitters in your brain, such as dopamine, serotonin and endorphins. Each release renders you craving more leading to greater achievements.

So, this book is, unequivocally, about you maximizing your potential. It suggests the point at which the basics end as the starting point for discussion of your ascension. It begins with an above average status and provides an easy to employ, common sense means for greater improvements. Utilizing a multitude of sound strategies, it makes a daunting endeavor simple by separating it into easily achievable tasks.

Although personal satisfaction is the central driver for overachievers, acquiring wealth is a measuring stick for many. In this vein, there is no doubt that many individuals in the United States have given significant attention to their finances. A recent Board of Governors of the Federal Reserve System Survey of Consumer Finances estimated that there are more than 7.6 million households with $2 million or more in net worth and 4.6 million households with a net worth of $3 million or more.[2] These persons have, from an economic vantage point, achieved above average outcomes.

Meanwhile, there are persons that fit the mold of the norm. They have reached mid-level leadership at their place of employment. They possess a decent home, two solid vehicles, a couple of children, and actively participate in their child's parent-teacher organization. This is their lifestyle and very little changes for decades while the world is evolving around them.

Mind you, this way of life is acceptable on seemingly all fronts. It is common, if not the beaten path. It is orthodox and connotes stability. Yet, it's simply the average level of achievement. It doesn't allow you to stand out. You tend to blend into the woodwork. You may delight in the virtues of life, but it doesn't break through many of the barriers to extraordinary progress. At this point, you are essentially a member of the pack, not the leader of it.

Why stop here? If you aspire to be more than average, address the fundamentals of life first. Yet, upon mastery be aware that this is only the beginning of your rise to preeminence.

The norm serves as a platform for your upward movement. Once you reach the norm, you are ready to shift from intermediate to advanced or from the middle to the top tier of achievement. Conceptually, this coincides with the precepts in this text. You must clearly identify and exceed average. With average bested, the discussion of moving to preeminent begins.

Although, we start each idea put forward in this text at a level of accomplishment that escapes many, it is apparent and irrefutable that anyone can be great. Yet, it must also be stated that anyone can, but not everyone will.

Throughout this book, there are anecdotes describing individuals who refuse to move the needle for their own lives. In these stories, there are persons who possess unique talents and skills, but fail to recognize or make use of countless resources afforded to them. In contrast, we discuss persons of similar intellect and ability that seize opportunities relentlessly. This difference is brought forward through research, interviews, observations and personal tales. The result is an amalgamation of methods that are proven to help you find success in any endeavor. Illustrations of numerous overachievers are also conveyed to aid you in reaching your next level of achievement and support reeling the goal of personal satisfaction closer and closer to you. Further, this book provides an extension of the success tools brought to bear in Volume I of this series.

Based on where you are on the continuum of from great to preeminent, the information shared here not only provides an intellectual and practical methodology for sharpening your success skill set, but is a catalyst for exponential leaps on your journey as an overachiever.

When put into practice daily, these teachings prepare you for adversity as you climb to higher rungs on your ladder of success. They also provide solutions to many of the common issues you will encounter in your ascension. Relevant research is combined with personal testimonials to convey clear guidance as you progress. When you lack follow through, this text gives you the mental tools to persevere. For the problem of you stopping short, it prods you to always exceed the standard.

All people, even the most talented in their field, need a motivational shot in the arm at some point. In an area in which their passion abounds, a dwindling of motivation can likely occur over time. Yet, a smidgeon of insight or inspiration can help them return to form and move beyond a barrier to which they have yielded continuously.

The $61 Day

For example, many years ago my wife and I opened our first retail business on a shoestring budget. We knew that it would be difficult, but decided that we would focus on keeping our personnel costs to a minimum to help the business survive while in its early stages. We had a solid grand opening. With a few techniques in place to build our clientele, we began to experience growth. My father, who owned multiple successful businesses, regularly visited our establishment. On one occasion after just a few days of operation, he stopped by and thoroughly looked around the facility. He asked a few pointed questions about sales, marketing and overhead costs. Before leaving, his advice to me was that if I just kept the doors open, it would be well worth it. I accepted his advice, but was shaken on a Tuesday three weeks into the endeavor. Having pledged to keep personnel costs low, my wife and I worked most of the hours while the retail store was open. I worked full-time in my vocation while she worked full-time in our retail business. On the Tuesday in question, I arrived at the business in early evening after a difficult day at my regular place of employment. My wife explained that sales had been very sluggish so far that day. As a matter of fact, that day was the worst we had experienced. I checked the receipts and was extremely disappointed. We had accumulated less than $50 in gross sales up to that point. I remained on site until closing and a few more patrons shopped, but for low dollar items. At closing, I calculated the day's receipts and they totaled only $61.87. I put my head down in disgust. The time, effort and money that had gone into establishing the business seemed to be for naught. I was very upset. As I closed the business for the night, I began to think about what my father told me. If I just kept the doors open, it would be well worth it. So, I wrapped it up for the night and stated to myself, we'll see what happens tomorrow. From that night forward, my wife and I decided to place a heavy focus on marketing. The next day, we experienced an exponential increase in sales and each day afterwards the business showed promise amidst some paltry days of sales. Years later, the business stabilized. It became very profitable; and, just keeping the doors open was worth it.

The story of the $61 day parallels many of the principles highlighted in this text. Although my father passed away only a few weeks after my wife and I opened the business, he imparted a success tool that steered us towards prosperity. What he wanted us to understand was that longevity is a key to creating a successful business.

Likewise, the messages in this book replicate the advice I was given on my road to achievement. I share these tools to help readers at seemingly any point in their progression accomplish their goals.

More specifically, the story of the $61 day addresses the doubt that you are likely to experience as you work to cross thresholds in your career or business. It highlights mental models and principles to guide you in pursuing wealth, improving your health or any quest that fits your liking. It also sheds a strong light on the notions of time, consistency, longevity and persistence as essential on your trek to surpass your previous levels of achievement. Overall, this personal narrative underpins the primary rationale of this text. The intent is to provide you with tools that allow you to accomplish any goal. In the process, you become the ideal version of yourself.

What must be evident from the $61day scenario is that we exist in a time in which anything that you conceive can be achieved. Yet, the most important factor is time. No matter where a person is on the talent spectrum, the willingness to continuously apply themselves over time is why anyone can do it, but everyone won't. In unabashed, unsugar-coated terms, you cannot quit.

Again, why are there more than 7 million households with more than $2 million in net worth in the America? It's because the doors of opportunity are not just open, but gaping. Capitalizing on these opportunities is much easier when the tested, proven success tools put forward in this book are employed.

In a sense, the innumerable people who squander opportunities or are not seeking to continuously advance are doing themselves, let alone their families, a disservice. This is because the blueprints for high achievement and realizing personal satisfaction are not only here in black and white, but easily accessible to most individuals. One need only read, adopt and employ the tools. For some, it is a failure to subscribe to a more progression-centered state of mind or to learn new skills. For others, it is a lack of planning on the front end of a pursuit that would allow them to reap tremendous rewards on the back end. For individuals who feel they have reached their zenith, there is still more to accomplish. These top performers should bear in mind that the room of achievement has unlimited square footage. There are multitudes of above average people who are not aware that their best performance to date in their area of passion is just so-so. Regardless of your current ability, even if you behold it as outstanding, you can still push past your ceiling.

Your Highest Jump

In that vein, on September 8, 1988 in Salamanca Spain, Cuban athlete Javier Sotomayor, set the world record for the high jump with a height of 2.43 m or 7' 11 ¾".[3] Knowing that his best at that juncture could be improved, Sotomayor continued to train. And, on July 29, 1989, in San Juan, Puerto Rico, he broke his own record with a height of 2.44 m or 8'. This achievement could have possibly remained the world record for decades, but Sotomayor could not rest on his laurels. Sotomayor realized that he held the two highest high jumps on record. With the proper training, time and effort his previous records could be eclipsed. Thus, on July 27, 1993, nearly four years later, in Salamanca, Spain, Sotomayor again broke his own world record with a height of 2.45 m or 8' ½".[4]

Javier Sotomayor is highlighted because his first, second and third world record jumps were achieved through unmatched forethought, time, effort and seamless execution. Sotomayor understood that even his best was not the summit, but a point on his journey to preeminence.

Know that Sotomayor's peak is exclusive to him and your top performance in a field of your own choosing is exclusive to you. I implore you to not leave your best years on the table when opportunity rests on the tips of your fingers. Don't allow yourself to misuse your treasure trove of opportunities due to self-doubt. You must remain keenly aware of its presence. Doubt is always lurking. But, when you trample it, when doubt is an enemy that you see coming and stamp it out before it has a chance to attack, a continually improving version of you emerges. You need only unceasingly exert yourself towards implementation of your ideas.

Countless people arise from their beds each morning and submit themselves to the same routine day after day. In many cases, the routine is progressive. Yet, even greater numbers of individuals are not aware that they are creatures of habit and, at best, just maintaining the status quo. Each morning, throngs of individuals shower in a rush, check their texts and emails, grab a steaming cup of classic roast coffee, nibble on a biscuit and fruit, give a good-bye kiss to their family and they're on their way to meet the schedule set by their employer. They never apply themselves toward a passion before 7 a.m., after 4 p.m. or on the weekends. They are simply exhausted following work and feel trapped in a state of this is all I can do. The idea that they are tired is fixed in their mind every single day upon arrival at home following work. Many others have ideas to extend themselves in their area of passion, but allow their self-proclaimed fatigue to engender fear, doubt and procrastination to the extent that they don't take steps to bring their ideas to fruition. This cycle disallows the ends to which their minds would like to carry them to ever be brought into existence.

There are also those persons whose only mode of operation is copying what their friends are doing. Their friends decide to purchase a pontoon boat and they break their bank by leasing a Boston Whaler 285 Conquest boat with cutting edge features.[5] Their buddies take an expensive trip to Laucala Island in Fiji.[6] They counter by expending thousands traveling to Bora Bora Island in French Polynesia.[7] It's you do; I do. There is absolutely nothing wrong with paying to partake in the enjoyment these luxuries can bring. Yet, if one is doing so only as a copycat or hasn't considered the consequences, I would advise them to rethink this approach. Even further, many people are imprisoned in a lifestyle that does not permit them to evolve intellectually or financially. They are simply carbon copies stagnated by keeping pace with others as opposed to grabbing life by the horns and steering it in a direction that is unique to them.

Let's be clear. It is one's prerogative how they spend their money or develop themselves as a person throughout life. It's a freedom we all possess. But, I would be neglectful if I didn't convey to you that life is a gold mine of sorts. Its treasures must be extracted and only you can dig them up for yourself. Why be satisfied with the minimum or just the basics? This is especially important to consider given that abundance and achievement do not discriminate.

What is transparent from this book is the notion that you can be more than mediocre and much more than great. Why sit smugly after a handful of wins or being bestowed a few trophies? Why rest on your laurels or sit on your hands?   Even if you are considerably above average in a field of work, this state can be bested. You can be preeminent. But, this esteemed level is not found in mirroring your friends or neighbors or an unchanging, non-progressive regimen.   It requires you to continuously cross thresholds, evolve as a person, employ a strong work ethic, possess an insatiable desire to achieve, and produce excellent results while leading as opposed to following.

In short, if you've had it with underachievement or a subpar version of yourself, then the following chapters will give you the rudiments of preeminence. The outcome will be you with not just all the bells and whistles, but an improved mindset that allows you to surpass any level of achievement you could have conceived possible in foresight. So, read, adopt each principle, share with your family and friends and enjoy your journey to the summit and in the likeness of Javier Sotomayor, you can achieve your highest jump. Good day to you.

INTRODUCTION

This book comprises six of E.M. Robinson's lectures including: I) *Crossing the Threshold*, II) *Evolve Your Main Asset*, III) *The Workaholic*, IV) *Never Satisfied*, V) *Bonus Lecture: *Strike a Nerve* and VI) *Bonus Lecture: *Stop Keeping up with the Joneses.*

Each lecture is a critical piece to the overarching notion of great to preeminent and provides myriad success tools for the overachiever. Following chapters I-IV, readers are encouraged to complete the reflection and practice sections to promote continued progress towards goal accomplishment.

In Chapter I, *Crossing the Threshold* is presented. This lecture provides four nuggets of wisdom to ensure that you have the tools to overcome the formidable foes of fear, doubt and procrastination. Making a decision and launching your plan immediately, augmenting your self-confidence, wise budgeting of your time and pursuing your obsession unrelentingly allow you to triumph any obstacle en route to accomplishment of your most compelling goals.

In Chapter 2, *Evolve Your Main Asset* is provided. This lecture outlines three tenets of self-improvement that take your body, mind and soul to levels beyond anything you could have comprehended beforehand. Combining the old with the new, enhancing your existing skills and giving to gain, illuminate your future elicit an improved mindset.

In Chapter 3, *The Workaholic* is shared. This lecture supplies a school of thought that informs you to stop squandering opportunities and always exceed the standard. These two concepts allow you to enjoy the capture of your greatest goals while enduring the chase.

In Chapter 4, *Never Satisfied* is put forward. This lecture imparts a manner of thinking including conviction, commitment and collaboration. These three Cs aid you in refining your persona, removing limits to your achievement and allow you to travel, both mentally and physically, to places that you didn't know existed.

The first bonus chapter is entitled *Strike a Nerve*. This lecture highlights the concepts of little things mean a lot, your goal is easy if you have a guide and over time you will learn to love the work that leads to accomplishment of your goal. These three pieces of intellect provide a jolt to your consciousness and spur you to a level of seriousness about your goals that yields unceasing activity and a new, more purposeful you.

In the second bonus chapter, the second iteration of *Stop Keeping up With the Joneses* is presented. This lecture draws attention to letting your imagination be your guide, becoming a sponge, mastering little money for big results, learning to stop trying to be all things to all people and your success is exclusive to you. These points of advice prod you towards an enviable level of focus in completion of your goals.

Chapter I

Crossing the Threshold

•INSPIRATION•

This lecture was inspired by Chef Everett Alan Robinson whose every move in life is geared toward crossing the threshold.

Chapter I

Lecture Title: Crossing the Threshold

Have you accomplished that big goal? Or, are you still procrastinating, waiting for the right time to act? If you've been delaying action or pushing aside your dreams, the time has come for you to cross the threshold.

I am not talking about just improving your mindset. I am referring to making decisions that change everything about you: the way you perceive yourself, the way others view you, your abilities and potential, your self-confidence, the way you walk, how you articulate your thoughts, your apparel and how you present yourself to others.

This is Dr. E.M. Robinson and I am supplying you with four nuggets of thought and action that allow you to cross the threshold of the old you and emerge into a new, more vibrant, exciting, dynamic and intentional version of yourself.

There is an old saying that no matter your lot in life, build something on it. Crossing the threshold equates to not only the start of construction on your foundation of achievement, but the actual completion of your goals. Regardless of the adversities you encounter, your reinvention requires you to cross the threshold.

You'll realize that your threshold is specific to you. It's personal and exclusively yours. But, most importantly, it is only a few steps away.

Since your threshold is nigh, I will give you four

strategies that I implore any person who holds personal development as one of their highest priorities to adopt and engage. This lecture will propel your movement and transformation into a new, kinetic, inspiring and prosperous version of yourself. First, we'll discuss making a decision and launching your plan immediately. Next, we'll address the intellectual strength builder-- augmenting your self-confidence. Third, we'll tackle wise budgeting of your time which is, at its core, central to a lifetime of continuous improvement and success. And, fourth we will peer into pursuing your obsession unrelentingly, one of the most essential components in crossing the threshold.

So, let's dissect these four points. This will give you an advantage when striving to overcome the formidable foes of fear, doubt and procrastination that tend to prevent large numbers of people from crossing the threshold.

Make a Decision and Launch Your Plan Immediately

My first call to action in this lecture is to address the foremost step in any extraordinary accomplishment. In terms of importance, nothing is more of a priority than the decision to make a change and launching your plan immediately. This is a most important point. All improvement stems from this moment.

To make this leap, I would first like you to consider the custom of jumping over the broom. This tradition represents an informal, not legally valid, agreement between a couple. It has a questionable history of references emerging from 18th century West African Ghana and 18th century England.[8] The practice was made popular in the 1970s through Alex Haley's novel and miniseries "Roots." With that background, envision crossing the threshold in the likeness of this custom when a man and woman were married, they jumped a broom to signify their union. The rest of the story ensues with the man picking up the woman and carrying her through the door of their abode to work together for a lifetime and resolve their issues as one. Making a decision and launching your plan immediately is equivalent. For couples, the threshold comes in deciding to tie the knot and not look back. This step can be a huge lift without the proper mindset. If self-doubt is abounding, instead of being able to lift the woman and carry the burdens that they both bear, the doubt is so unwieldy that the woman cannot be carried nor can either of them fit through the door. For others, it is their fear and procrastination that disallows them to jump over the broom. They wait unendingly for the right time, but it never arrives. Due to their inaction, they never officially bring their union to fruition. Hence, the decision to make the change is the first and primary step in crossing the threshold; it yields a new direction, a fresh start and the initial energy and optimism to take you through the early challenges.

Furthermore, the decision to simply take the first step triggers the launch; this is a critical time for you in your development and progression. If you commit to starting your dream business, you cannot allow the ideas to remain in your head, that is if you want real, hard, fast achievement. The ideas must be extracted from your mind right away and placed in black and white. From the mental model comes the physical, so the idea must be formed theoretically and subsequently put into action to be concrete. In short, write your ideas down when they are conceived.

Once your ideas are on paper, you can truly begin to cross the threshold because the decision to act in a given manner is your launch pad. This equates to ridding yourself of psychological burdens that block you from deciding what you are willing to give in return for the outcomes you desire.

Launching my Second Retail Establishment

Several years back, I was in an optimal position financially and psychologically to start my second retail establishment. The idea had been lingering for years, but I didn't pull the trigger because I felt the time wasn't right. One evening after work, I arrived home and my wife told me she needed to talk to me about something very serious. She informed me that her position at work was being eliminated or at minimum reduced to a less than gainful wage. So, I immediately mentioned the retail idea that we discussed from time to time. We pondered the idea in earnest and decided to launch immediately. We drew up the business plan. Through extensive legwork and research: contacting the state department of revenue, prospective vendors, surveying potential customers, assessing costs, time and effort, we constructed a model for the business that we were confident would work. It was a blue-chip idea, so we went with it. We didn't allow grass to grow up around our ideas and plans. We immersed ourselves in bringing the ideas to fruition. Although it was a daunting task to start, once we became mired in the details of its development, we found even greater energy and were delighted to put in the time and concentration to see our ideas realized. After a few years, we began to see the fruits of our labor. To this day, we are happy that we made the decision.

What one must know is that definitively deciding straightway to accomplish a goal is like striking a match and applying it to dry kindling. You first make the decision with conviction. You follow the decision with a commitment to a course of action. And, finally, you engage yourself relentlessly as your dreams and the world open to you.

So, decide now what you will accomplish. Act on it immediately. This can bridge the gap between almost and entirely in your life's book of accomplishments.

Build Your Self-confidence

The second notion that I urge you to consider in crossing the threshold is to build your self-confidence. Orison Swett Marden, in his seminal work, *He Can Who Thinks He Can*, urges individuals to increase their self-confidence as the means for accomplishing anything they conceive.[9] If you think you can build it, you can build it.

If you think you can succeed, you can succeed. The catalyst for accomplishment lies in belief. One of my deceased brothers, Eugene II, a man of substance, rendered these words to me while bedridden and afflicted with a dangerous kidney disease just a few days prior to his death. He said "Ed, it doesn't matter what it is. You can do anything you put your mind to." It sounds simple, but let's peer into this more deeply. Alexandra Sifferlin in *Time Health* boasts of recent studies showing that self-confidence is more than an emotion and is quantifiable.[10] There is even a study that puts forward the idea that Harvard graduates succeed not because they are more talented than others, although many possess outstanding proclivities in given areas, but because they are extremely confident in their abilities.[11]

Confidence gives you the impetus to accomplish things that those who are not endowed with confidence are unable to do. Your self-confidence is a tool and weapon and can break down barriers for you when others are stymied. Confidence is the game breaker, the injection that yields positive results and the ingredient that makes the dish delectable. Confidence overcomes fear, doubt, and procrastination. Confidence gets the promotion because confidence makes you volunteer for the difficult projects. Confidence keeps you from being overlooked because you are coveted for your ability and your willingness to accomplish tasks. Confidence hits a grand slam, makes the perfect throw or sinks the bucket in the clutch. Confidence is the attribute that allows you to cross threshold after threshold in your life and makes the risk seem like a sure thing in hindsight. Confidence is the characteristic that allows you to redouble your actions and to multiply your efforts even in the face of adversity. Confidence can be likened to a mustard seed, as expressed in the parable in the book of Matthew, that when sowed into a field although smaller than all seeds grows greater than herbs and becomes a tree, so that the birds of the air come and lodge in its branches.[12]

Building self-confidence, at first glance, seems small, but is a key to your advancement and can be ameliorated using the approach put forward by Lewis Howes in Forbes magazine.[13] Howes suggests that the key to great accomplishments is thinking small initially. When you knock out the small goals first, this builds confidence for increasingly greater feats over time. And with numerous accomplishments under your belt, it gives you the psychological advantage to take on and accomplish larger goals.

If he were alive, U.S. president, Theodore Roosevelt, would be inclined to state to you that "each time we face our fear; we gain strength, courage, and confidence in the doing."[14]

I encourage any person who holds self-improvement as a top priority to work on their self-confidence as it closes the chasm between thinking and doing. And, again I state in even more transparent terms that if you are working in your vocation and would like to soar to the top of your organization, I suggest that you show confidence by volunteering to lead an initiative. In the words of Orison Swett Marden, a volunteer makes a better soldier than a drafted man.[15]

In short, exercising leadership increases your confidence and eventually you are too great in skills and mind to be confined to your current position. Put bluntly, your ascension is imminent.

Being a Confident School Administrator

More than ten years ago, I was an entry-level school administrator making my mark in the field. I was pursuing a terminal degree and developing a sense of mastery of my craft. On one occasion, a more seasoned, entry-level, but retirement-ready administrator accosted me. I am not sure if it was done in jest, but I addressed it. This administrator had served in the same role for many years. He seemed to show a little envy to me possibly because of my vim and youth. One day, he came into my office and said Mr. Robinson, I see that you lift weights, and you think you are tough. When I was your age, I could kick your ass. I quickly retorted, "well come on then; do it now." He replied softly "nah, I'm not going to bother you this time." Although a tad comical, this scenario was an exhibition of my self-confidence. It goes without saying that the seasoned administrator never challenged me again and was extremely respectful from that moment forward.

The China Mentality

Not long ago, I viewed a presentation discussing

the success of Chinese immigrants versus other ethnic groups in the United States. In the presentation, the narrator stated that Chinese immigrants are more successful than whites and blacks with the same IQ not because they are inherently better, but because of their work ethic.[16]   Their work ethic engrains the confidence to work unceasingly until they have achieved success. This China mentality in few words is, if anybody can do it, let it be us.

Confidence is essential to crossing the threshold and I implore you to build yours to the level of an Ivy League graduate or all-star professional athlete. And, if anyone is going to accomplish what others have not, like the Chinese, let it be you.

Use Your Time Wisely

In these talks, we've discussed the notion that it is a universal law that all things change over time. The third piece of advice that I offer you in relation to crossing the threshold is to use your time wisely. Time is a critical factor; and, since all things change over time whether you apply yourself, capitalize on your potential or squander opportunities, you should focus on prudence in the budgeting of your time. Why not use these seconds, minutes, hours, days, months and years with sagacity and precision? Change will come regardless of your level of mental or physical exertion. Your energy levels, stamina, desires and priorities will change over time anyway, so wise use of time is one of the secrets to you crossing thresholds to high achievement.

Even the sun, albeit it has shone for 4.57 billion years and based on scientists' estimates has about 4.5-5.5 billion years remaining, will exhaust its supply of hydrogen and helium and collapse into a white dwarf.[17] The moon even waxes and wanes over the course of a 28-day period: from New moon to Waxing Crescent, First Quarter, Waxing Gibbous, Full moon, Waning Gibbous, Third Quarter and Waning Crescent.[18] Einstein in his theory of relativity imparts that all motion is relative and uses time as a fourth dimensional space.[19] You can't control time, but you do possess autonomy over your motion, so employ it wisely.

Since time is the single most critical factor in your success, I am compelled to inform you to find a means for spending as much time as possible in stimulating environments. From school to those you befriend, your success rides largely on the environment you place yourself in. A recent study of students who, at minimum, visit a college campus during their early life shows that a high percentage of those students attend and graduate from college versus their counterparts who have not spent any time on a college campus.[20] In this regard, being exposed to and engaging those who show ambition will prod you along. Spending time in a stimulating environment can be an impetus to your greatness. Ken Griffey, Sr. and Jr. along with a host of father-son professional athletes show that the time they spend immersed in an apt environment can lead to outstanding individual outcomes.

To be clear, using time wisely is simply conventional wisdom. Learning to manage your time, especially as you pursue great accomplishments, is critical to success.

A few years back, I was on the cusp of completing a terminal degree, worked daily in my vocation, operated and managed multiple businesses, contributed to local civic organizations, maintained a wholesome marriage, and routinely engaged family and friends. This multitude of endeavors required me to work long hours, unselfishly commit time, energy and funds to a cause while still availing myself to my wife, children and friends. Initially, this multitude of tasks was daunting, but desire defeated fatigue and management of time allowed me to satisfy my desires. I broke my life into smaller steps. I focused more on organization and preparation than the actual actions comprising any tasks. This led to ease and fluidity of my work. The load was still great, but I budgeted my time wisely. I prepared and planned my meals, spent more time organizing my thoughts before meetings, read thoroughly, took copious notes and ensured that my task lists included personal items such as dinner with the wife, golf with my son or watching a movie with my daughter. The result was the ability to juggle the most important aspects of life while accomplishing many large projects. Clearly, this was due in large part to time budgeting, but more specifically, breaking life down into smaller steps.

The notion of using time wisely is best illustrated by the fable of the ant and the grasshopper.[21] The ant worked diligently to store up resources while they were plentiful. In contrast, the grasshopper sang and played. When winter came, bringing with it snow and little resources, the grasshopper had nothing stored away while the ant had plenty. When the grasshopper sought the ant to request resources, the ant rebuked the grasshopper's idleness and turned it away to face the cold of winter. From this fable of Aesop, it is abundantly clear that wise use of time allows you to not only cross the threshold, but overachieve.

Prudent budgeting of your time is a success tool that reels greatness closer to you each day and places preeminence on your radar for future attainment. Hence, I urge all slackers, those immersed in mediocrity, business startups, fledgling professionals, and even seasoned veterans to give attention to their use of time. From adoption of an approach that focuses heavily on wise use of time, the extraordinary life you are seeking will be attained and you will be the inspiration that others seek on their journey to preeminence.

Pursue Your Obsession Unrelentingly

We've burrowed into making a decision and launching your plan immediately, adding to your self-confidence and prudent use of time. Yet, I would be neglecting an essential piece in imparting advice toward your advancement if I failed to address pursuing your obsession unrelentingly. There is something that we all must have in this life and our lives are seemingly incomplete without it. Let's call that something X. For some, X is as simple as a three-bedroom house with a large backyard for family use. For others, X is the founding of a global corporation with double-digit billions in revenue. No matter what X is, you must pursue it with every iota of energy and intellect that you possess. If you want X, you can have X, but acquiring X requires endless dogged determination. Once you have decided what your X is, you must overcome any stumbling block to possess it.

What you must know about X is that it might require you to commit to a sustained effort over an extended time. This could be many months, years or multiple decades. As well, accomplishment of X might feature a major nemesis that beats you time and time again. Yet, you realize that X is on the other side of defeating your nemesis.

If highly celebrated poet, Robert Frost, were speaking to you about acquiring X, he would aptly inform you that the best way out is always through.[22] The application of this maxim with respect to acquiring X is, in one word, persistence. The first known use of persistence is 1546 and it remains applicable in your life today if you are seeking to bring X into existence.[23]

X is within a stone's throw and across the chasm of decision making, building your confidence and properly managing your time. X is standing right in front of you. You can almost taste it; you can see it clearly. But, you cannot possess X unless you pursue it without ceasing.

In unambiguous terms, possessing, embracing or experiencing X, requires you to covet X as if your life and sanity depends on it. A burning, unquenchable desire to grab hold of, embody or reach X must exist within you. It is essential to view X as not being able to be considered X anymore without you achieving it. X is behind the door of opportunity and you must take the steps to enter through this door to meet X because X is on the other side of the threshold. You must know unequivocally that you cannot cross the threshold to your goal unless you pursue X nonstop.

My Ex-Girlfriend's X

I ran into a former girlfriend who I had not seen in nearly twenty years. She aspired to work in medicine from the day that I met her. I can unequivocally state that practicing medicine was and is her X as she discussed it in seemingly every conversation we had prior to her achieving it. Yet, from what I know about her past, she had some difficulty, including being beset early by negative decisions with drugs and noncomplementary companions. When I saw her recently, she had a special glow. As we conversed, she immediately informed me of her current undertakings. I was impressed. She had become a nurse and acquired a master's degree. She was also only a few months removed from receiving her doctorate and was now a nurse practitioner. She had gone from a common name to being addressed with an honorific. Her *X* had become a reality and she had crossed the threshold into a more dynamic version of herself.

Classic Examples of Pursuing an Obsession Unrelentingly

Henry Ford pursued the eight-cylinder engine unrelentingly and became one of the greatest industrialists of all time.[24] Michael Phelps chose to never cease working at his craft as a competitive swimmer leading to him being the most successful and decorated Olympian of all time.[25] Because he never relented, Phelps has an astounding, twenty-eight total medals, twenty-three of which are gold and eight in a single Olympics in 2008 in Beijing. Walt Disney's relentlessness as pioneer of the American animation industry, led him to possess the record for individual Academy Awards, having won 22 Oscars from 59 nominations.[26] Entrepreneur, investor, media magnate and founder of the Black Entertainment Television network, Robert Louis Johnson, became America's first African American billionaire because he did not relent in pursuing his obsession.[27] These are only a handful of individuals whose commitment, drive and temerity led to preeminence in their field.

The room of preeminence is vacant to us all if we seek what we desire until it is acquired. I urge all people who are interested in maximizing their potential to pursue their goals without fail. It can be this pursuit that allows you to embrace *X* having crossed a multitude of thresholds. From this unyielding focus on your goal, you will be laying the foundation for you to not only move into a different sphere of achievement, but be a name synonymous with excellence in your field.

Summary

Let's convert crossing the threshold into a pill that is easy to swallow. Making a decision, launching your plan immediately, increasing your self-confidence, using your time wisely and an obsessive pursuit of your X allows you to accomplish that big goal sooner rather than later. When you take the first step, everything about you begins to change. Your self-confidence grows when you accomplish small goals. These small accomplishments instill within you the confidence to take on increasingly larger and more fulfilling goals. You begin to realize that time budgeting is essential to maintaining your progress toward X as the ardency of your pursuit intensifies. You are on the proper trajectory. Your ascension is imminent. There is no stumbling block too unwieldy to be moved and there are no nemeses that you cannot overwhelm and defeat.

This has been Dr. E. M. Robinson with *Crossing the Threshold.* I urge you to decide right now what your X will be. Make haste to bring X to pass. You will increase your self-confidence each step of the way, organize your minutes, days and hours to increase your productivity and approach your goal without relenting. When you have crossed the threshold, you will embrace X while becoming a new, more dynamic you. Good day to you.

Crossing the Threshold Reflection & Practice

Instructions:

Answer the following questions honestly and thoroughly and review your responses daily. Helpful tip: Copy your responses and post them in a location you will be apt to view each day (e.g., bathroom mirror).

1. Having internalized the significance of making a decision and launching your plan immediately, in 3-5 sentences discuss a plan in business, your vocation or other area of your life that would engender personal satisfaction when acted upon. (*e.g., My goal is to be founders of a condiment production and packaging corporation that distributes to restaurant supply stores in a tristate area. The array of condiments that this company will produce...*)

_____
_____
_____
_____
_____
_____
_____
_____
_____
_____

Note: Immediately after you have placed this plan on paper, do not hesitate any longer. Start today taking the first steps in your plan. See this plan through to realize a new, more dynamic version of yourself.

2.Considering that building self-confidence is critical to you crossing thresholds on the path to your highest achievements, in 2-3 sentences discuss one lofty goal that you have allowed to escape you thus far and the reasons for it not being accomplished. Next, list the first and easiest step towards its accomplishment and act on this step immediately (*e.g., I have drawn up a business plan for producing and packaging an array of condiments for distribution to restaurant supply stores in a tristate area. Yet, I have allowed my plan to collect dust because I haven't been creative in gathering the capital and resources to launch this company. Today, I will begin perfecting my recipes and branding materials...*)

_____

_____

_____

_____

_____

_____

_____

_____

_____

_____

Note: Once you take this first step, you will be closer to achieving your goal. Execute the remaining steps one-by-one and you will see your goal take shape.

3.Having worked on the notion of prudent use of your time, in 3-5 sentences explain the adjustments you will make in life to ensure that you are spending an increasingly greater amount of time in stimulating environments. (*e.g., My aunt is an attorney and physician who owns two retail establishments. Our conversations have always been stimulating and her accomplishments are impressive. I will deliberately and consistently spend time engaging her by occasionally visiting her in evenings following work or inviting her to dine out or have coffee.)*

_____
_____
_____
_____
_____
_____
_____
_____

Note: Refer to Chapter 2, Action 3 in Volume I of this book series to revisit daily goal setting tools.

4. Pursuing your obsession without ceasing is your means for acquiring X (the one accomplishment or acquisition that makes your life fulfilling). In 3-5 sentences, discuss your X and explain in big picture terms the time frame and obstacles you must overcome to access your X. (e.g., *My X is to become the president of a community college in the northeastern United States. It is sure to require at least 10 years of postsecondary leadership experience, i.e., professorship, tenure, work as a dean and or vice-president of academic affairs. One of the obstacles that I will face will be ensuring that I produce numerous, respected scholarly works each year. These are important rungs on which I must step on the ladder to the position of college president.)*

_____

_____

_____

_____

_____

_____

_____

_____

_____

_____

Bonus Reflection & Practice: Mantra Development

Develop a one sentence mantra that illustrates your mindset and mode of operation in relation to goal accomplishment. Be sure that this mantra is action-centered and reflects what you are committed to display as your personality for a lifetime. (*e.g., As long as you don't quit, you cannot fail.*)

_____

_____

_____

_____

_____

Chapter II

Evolve Your Main Asset

Chapter II

Lecture Title: Evolve Your Main Asset

Are you still doing the same things you did 10 years ago? Same old routine; same results? Are you working in the same position with the same salary and the same turkey and cheese sandwich for lunch every Wednesday? Why? Explain why you've remained stagnant.

When you were 25, you had grandiose dreams of what you would do and what you would become. You possessed endless energy, but now 15 years later, you speak only of retirement and no mention of the education you planned to attain, the places you wanted to visit or live or the businesses you desired to start to bring about your prosperity. If you've settled, if you've given up, I can only shake my head because I'm keenly aware that you have greater potential than what you currently display and remarkable outcomes awaiting you if you just consider your main asset.

What must be understood is that this main asset is very close to you. You use it unconsciously. But, before we define your main asset, let's address a few notions. Think about it. You've been giving to your employer for years. What about you? Have you been adding to your personal satisfaction bottom line? What about making you prosper as opposed to your employer? What about educating yourself and arranging to travel to the places you always wanted to go? What about your psychological well-being versus your employer's finances or annual results? Well, if you haven't evolved your main asset, your evolvement starts today.

This is Dr. E.M. Robinson and I am offering you three means for ensuring that you have a full, developed, entertaining and cultivated life experience. What I am offering is designed to help you take hold of personal satisfaction and relish the irreplaceable gift of the minutes, hours and days that you have at your disposal.

Ostensibly, you can do as you wish with your remaining days. Yet, I implore you, especially if nothing has improved for you in years, to learn to evolve your main asset. I want you to allow this to sink in deeply, so it becomes a part of your being over time. I am first rendering you an aphorism that I have found to be profound in my travels and work. Here it is in raw form: One cannot see the future without going forward. This maxim is presented because it's common sense; it's unambiguous and logical. You cannot see your opportunities outside unless you open the door. In layman's terms, a closed mouth cannot be fed.

There are numerous cases in everyone's life in which they were summoned to engage in a new experience with the propensity to bring excellent gain, but they rejected it. It could have been as simple as tasting a dish that you had avoided for a lifetime. Yet, had you tried the dish, you would have not just enjoyed it, but considered it the most delectable food you had ever tasted. Although this tasty dish scenario seems inconsequential, let's peer into this notion more deeply.

Something as simple as a dish could lead to you making that food for your personal consumption. You like the dish so much that this leads to you to tweak the recipe. The new version is so remarkable that it's market worthy and thus a business opportunity with seemingly indefinite value. Just one taste, can produce positive results. Hence, one cannot see the future without moving forward.

There have been many more significant instances such as when you were invited to attend a social event, but declined. You sat at home watching television. Sure, the movie you watched was entertaining and the popcorn hit the spot, but you missed an opportunity to meet the one company representative who would have been impressed with your passion and verve and invited you to interview for a new, dynamic and lucrative position. Again, one cannot see the future without moving forward.

In some cases, this means taking a shot, climbing through the window of opportunity or anticipating a niche and filling it. That long-awaited break or day when that posting for your dream position is made is always on the horizon.

To be clear, it is difficult to make advancements when you're stuck in the present. Especially, as there are times when we don't realize that each day that passes becomes the past. Even an immaculate home becomes stale if you never let any air inside. You can't see the future without moving forward.

To illustrate this point further, I provide three notions to help evolve your main asset and keep you from losing your freshness. First, is combining the old with the new. Second, is enhancing your existing skills. And, third is giving to gain. If you're even remotely interested in improving your life to the tune of extraordinary results, I encourage you to adopt these three principles for evolving your main asset.

Combine the old with the new

The first order of business in evolving your main asset is to know with certitude what comprises your main asset, but also to learn to combine the old with the new as a means for advancement. Your main asset is not foreign to you if you are paying attention. And, combining the old with the new is the method for improvement in nearly every life circumstance. In the classic text, *Competing for the Future*, Gary Hamel and C.K. Prahalad discuss new age tools for remaining competitive in business.[28] These authors speak to the notion of the hybrid--the blending of the old with the new to bring about amelioration. These are the same tools for rendering yourself competitive across all facets of life. Even in Behr and Nohria's blockbuster publication, *Breaking the Code of Change*, the message is similar, if not identical to Hamel and Prahalad's. Behr and Nohria decree that staying relevant in business is a function of fusing the past with the present. From these two pundits in industry, the prescription is the same for continuous improvement and relevance; the mode of operation must be to combine the old with the new.[29]

New innovations from old capabilities have always

been the catalyst for improvement.[30] For example, the Sholes typewriter was the result of synthesis of numerous extant mechanical technologies. Together these applications of knowledge engendered something novel and captivating. In addition, early electronics fused with small electric motors and manual typewriters created a new machine, the personal computer. This quantum leap in technology carried with it the old and familiar QWERT keyboard and other typing conventions. The personal computer itself was constructed from extant components from other areas of the electronics industry. This includes TV monitors, printed circuit boards, memory chips, semiconductors, etc.

This is evidence that combining the old with the new allows you to expand, to stretch and be refined while remaining cutting-edge. A music connoisseur is only so because they understand and can play or compose music across many genres and time frames. A doctor's craft is limited if they only possess knowledge of the best medical practices of the past decades. A head coach in professional sports will soon be out of a job if they are not apprised of the most recent innovations and techniques for ensuring that individual players and teams are operating at their peak performance. In each of these cases, the professional must constantly adjust to remain relevant in the future. Combining the old with the new ensures that your mind and actions are aligned with the notion that the future is happening now.

Additionally, just because an item is aged doesn't mean it's time to completely discard it. How about integrating it into your existing systems? It just might be the component that sets your product apart from others. Some items that have in so many words, a few miles on them, perform the best or are the most useful and appropriate for a given application. Just consider many of the adages that span thousands of years and record and continue to be used because they never cease to be relevant. For instance, a penny saved is a penny earned. You don't miss your water until your well runs dry. It's a poor dog that won't wag its own tail. If you want your spot in the sun, you must be willing to deal with some blisters. There are many called, but only a few chosen. Aren't these maxims just as relevant now as when they were first uttered?

I encourage anyone intent upon excelling to internalize and adopt each of these maxims. I am sure that you will find that once you subscribe to each aphorism that your understanding of the world will become more refined. You will also retain your sophistication and prosper amidst the rapid evolution of society.

Understand that combining the old and new ushers you not only into greatness, but allows you to secure your place as preeminent. Several years back, I was tasked with the responsibility to move a chronically underperforming organization into a new phase of excellence. This position required the best of my leadership skills: vision, team building, positive thinking, purpose-driven actions and developing a problem-solving mindset and culture amongst other characteristics. Yet,

I can place a feather in my team's cap due in large part to the seamless fusion of our youthful and seasoned experiences and talent. The young, gung-ho leaders brought contemporary ideas to bear. They possessed endless energy and hammered out assignments like a machine. The more seasoned leaders explicated wisdom and their abundant resources supported our plunge into a future of excellence. This combination of newfangled approaches and tried and true methods allowed us to augment our outcomes exponentially.

Hence, if you are to overachieve, reaching the summit will require a blend of what has proven itself to be effective over time and modern ideas and tools that engender your evolution. In short, mixing the old with the new will keep your main asset from sitting idle; you will see the future because you will always be moving forward.

Enhance and Expand Your Existing Skills

Combining the old with the new is a starter of greatness and has immeasurable value, yet it is only a skeleton without the sinew of enhancing your existing skills. Improvements in your ability result in increases in performance. In fact, developing highly sought-after skills makes you more indispensable. This concept should resonate with any individual seeking to be elevated to the top of their organization. For example, having the information technology skills to perform high-level technical functions in your vocation makes you employable.	Adding	superior	communications, interpersonal, organizational, strategic planning and profit maximization talent will make you coveted.

Put simply, if you add a certification, acquire a new license, secure a permit, develop your technical knowledge, learn a new software program or attain a higher academic credential, not only have you expanded your faculties, but you have increased your value.

For a more in-depth look, let's just say you're a food inspector or environmentalist at a state or federal health agency. With minimal effort, you add a certification such as registered sanitarian or food safety specialist. Just this single addition makes you more skilled, increases your marketability and allows you to command a higher salary. You can rest assured that when internal positions become available that you can easily be in the running for that new corner office space with a personal restroom. Similarly, you can acquire an advanced degree in occupational, environmental or public health and be eligible for higher positions in the organizational structure. From this one add-on, more responsibility and greater comprehension are the likely result. Because you are now properly credentialed to teach at the collegiate level or be a consultant in your area of expertise, your skill sets you up for new, exciting and possibly lucrative opportunities.

Many years ago, I had an opportunity to take up piano while pursuing an undergraduate degree. I had no classes between the hours of 10:00 a.m. to 1:00 p.m. on Tuesdays and Thursdays. At the same time, the charitable organization of which I was an active member sought a musician. Thus, I decided to expand my extant music skill through two courses in piano instruction. After several months of development, I took these skills to the charity and provided them at no cost. Not only was I more valuable because of this evolution of my main asset, but I became a benefactor to the organization as I rendered music at no cost for decades.

If the American singer, songwriter, record producer and multi-instrumentalist, Anthony J. D'Angelo, were to discuss enhancing your existing skills, he would encourage you to, "become addicted to constant and never-ending self-improvement."[31] From this advice, you can be assured that expanding what you currently possess is a surefire means for advancement. This skill enhancement can be seen on display on a small scale seemingly everywhere you look, that is, if you are paying attention. Even Megan Gibson, who had always been a peanut butter lover, expanded her existing skills upon sampling a spicy Haitian variety. Once Gibson began creating her own recipes, she received rave reviews which led to her selling the spread at farmers' markets and other spots in Philadelphia. Because of this skill development she was led to purchase a food truck and launch PB & Jams which is a company she runs part-time while working full-time as a high school health teacher.[32]

I say to you that enhancing and expanding your existing skills is not difficult. It requires you to focus intently on developing yourself. Employing this mindset allows your ongoing improvement to remain facile as you are constantly using the attributes and resources that you already possess. If you are highly skilled in culinary arts, I encourage you to showcase this talent for profit, at minimum, in a single restaurant. The learning acquisition associated with becoming a restaurateur can be the mental stretch you require to become fulfilled as a person. This doesn't even venture into the notion of franchising or the construction of a factory that produces your cuisine for the masses. Once again, it is the simple, easy expansion of your existing skills that yields outstanding results. It is this slight shift in thought and behavior that helps you to move into the realm of great and on toward preeminence.

When I explain that you must enhance your existing skills, I am referring to knowing what is exceptional about you. Applying yourself toward the accentuation of this extraordinary characteristic must become your mode of operation. Just know that the grass is not greener on the other side; it's greener on your side.

Correspondingly, many corporations have come to realize that it is necessary to have as a standard operating procedure to hire from within. Employing this practice has produced spikes in productivity and creativity in the organization. The utilization of extant talent more so than external hiring is equivalent to the precept of enhancing and expanding your existing skills and its results are profoundly positive for organizations. When companies such as FedEx or Chick-fil-A hire their own, they are investing in resources that they already have. Not only is it easier, but it reduces the learning curve as the employee is already a part of the fabric of the organization.

When I implore you to use what you already have at your disposal as a means for reaching new levels, I am simply referring to your current characteristics and resources. To be clear and simple, build upon and maximize what can readily see and touch and especially that which you are currently using.

In my early twenties and fresh out on my own, I lived in an apartment complex with many tenants. There seemed to be so many children residing there. I noticed that they would walk great distances to stores in the area. So, I saw this as a business opportunity. Because of my lengthy experience in retail sales, I decided to create a small convenient store selling many of the items that tenants would walk long distances to purchase. I generated a substantial clientele in a short period and saw remarkable profits almost immediately. It was this experience that led me to much larger scale retail businesses. Thus, I give much credit to the notion of expanding my existing skills to the many of the successes that I have enjoyed as an entrepreneur.

Clearly, enhancing and expanding your existing skills speaks to simplicity and ease of improvement. If you're part of a growing corporation, the answer to a personnel dilemma of not being able to move up might be availing yourself to a project in the office down the hall or honing your skills out in the field as part of the sales team. Just look for the opportunities that are close and readily available. If you are seeking to rise to a higher position in your vocation, instead of waiting for the promotion, lure it to you by way of acquiring a certification, new skill, degree or showing initiative through taking on or volunteering to lead a new task. Basically, if you are seeking to move beyond average, fully use what you currently have at your disposal. This is the foremost means for evolving your main asset. You won't be sitting in that same office for a decade rotting away in stagnation or maxed out at the development of a single franchise. You will be a mover and shaker with constantly increasing market value.

Learn to Give to Gain

We've addressed combining the old with the new and enhancing your existing skills to an extent that provides at least two success tools for the overachiever. Yet, a third and final instrument of intellect and action must be proposed to aid in evolving your main asset. This last concept is learning to give to gain.

Although these lectures are not designed to promote religion of any sort, this topic is underpinned by a basic biblical principle. In Matthew 7:7 it reads: "Ask, and it shall be given you; seek, and ye shall find; knock, and it shall be opened unto you." In other words, the initial move is yours. You must take the first step. If you are not in the position you would like to be in, change it. If it's a higher compensated role, don't expect it to just pop up at your desk while you twiddle your thumbs. Jobs don't just show up to your place of residence, knock on the door and when you ask, 'who is there?' it responds: "job." You must apply yourself. Stop wishing; act. Sow profusely so that you can reap in abundance. Even Isaac Newton wanted us all to be keenly aware of this precept with his third universal law stating, "for every action, there is an equal and opposite reaction."[33] A parallel to this law is that for every inaction, there is an equal and opposite inaction. Therefore, your action is the key to receiving.

Giving to gain is a simple concept that we all should subscribe to if we're intent upon evolving our main asset. Even large corporations realize that they must give to gain. This can be illustrated by reviewing the concept of corporate social responsibility or CSR.[34] CSR ensures that companies conduct their business in an ethical manner. As a standard operating procedure, human rights, social, environmental and economic impacts should be accounted for when making decisions. This might involve activities such as partnering with local communities, making socially responsible investments, fostering relationships with customers and employees or promoting environmental protection. The outcome of these corporate actions is building trust with customers who continuously buy their products. Note, these measures help increase profits.

Giving to gain can be found in so many walks of life. From much research on parenting, we find that the primary means for rearing children to be precocious, good decision makers is not to constantly purchase them expensive material items, but to simply spend quality time with them.[35] Giving time to children more so than "stuff" profits parents and children alike. In most cases the result is learned, caring, conscientious children. And, any parent will tell you that having children who excel is of greater value to them than money. Not to mention, it provides a few bragging rights.

Just know that giving to gain is found throughout our world and should become a component in your personal school of thought if you desire to evolve your main asset. You can't pattern yourself after the parsimonious Uncle Scrooge or be closefisted and expect generosity to be returned to you. Life is not all take and no give.

In Aesop's fable, the Ant and the Dove, the ant found itself in a difficult situation, drowning in a puddle.[36] The dove provided a leaf as a lifeboat. Immediately after saving the ant, a hunter captured the dove in a net. The ant saw the dove in this difficult situation and bit the hunter on the foot. The hunter jumped in surprise and dropped the net allowing the dove to escape. The moral of this story is one good turn deserves another.

Again, you must give to gain. It is the tiniest of actions on your part that provide the greatest bang. Just think about a simple smile. It seems like a small and insignificant action, but when we study what it produces in return, you realize its value. A smile induces the release of the feel-good neurotransmitters in your body.[37] Dopamine, endorphins, and serotonin secretions are the outgrowth of a smile. These releases can make the difficult seem facile. A smile can bring about the antithesis of a foul mood. In a meeting, a smile can turn a negative aura positive. During a business transaction, a smile can seal the deal.

As a former school district leader, I worked in a setting in which turnover was extremely high. Giving to gain, my district began to offer packages that allowed educators to receive reimbursement for courses taken while seeking higher credentials. These same individuals would sign on for many years and proudly serve our students with no thoughts of leaving the district. Providing these small incentives allowed our district to knock a major dent in our turnover enigma.

Even innovation theory explains that business cycles are the result of new methods, new ideas, new tools or means of accomplishing tasks.[38] For businesses to stay atop their industry, remain relevant or outlast the competition, they must give to gain.

So, be apt to give. Be eager to take the first step. Your returns will be so great that a simple smile won't ever leave your face.

Summary

At this point, we have analyzed combining the old with the new, enhancing your existing skills and learning to give to gain. Consequently, your main asset should be as clear as a glass of tap water. But, just in case you remain unaware of your main asset, let me spell it out for you. Your main asset is your mind. Your mind will allow you to combine the old with new to produce a hybrid.

Evolution of this main asset will engender an extension of your extant skills and ensure that you are more marketable and increase your value. Finally, this advancement of your main asset motivates you to ask, seek and find outcomes beyond anything you could have conceived in advance.

This has been Dr. E.M. Robinson with *Evolve Your Main Asset.* As a closing thought, I encourage you to fuse the old and new, enhance your existing skills and give so that you are open to gain. And, the results of advancing your mind will allow you to produce such extraordinary results that you can't contain your smile. Good day to you.

Evolve Your Main Asset Reflection & Practice

Instructions:

Answer the following questions honestly and thoroughly and review your responses daily. You are encouraged to copy your responses and post them in a location you will be apt to view each day.

1. Combining the old with the new never ceases to be a means for advancement. In 3-5 sentences, explain a skill, idea, tool or method that you will blend with a new concept to revolutionize your life. (e.g., *In my vocation, I routinely conduct professional trainings in workshops at conferences around the country. During each presentation, I usually have the trainees produce handiwork specific to their companies only. After learning of the think-pair-share method, it is my plan to merge this tool with my current approach to ensure that the trainings are more engaging and collaborative.*)

_____
_____
_____
_____
_____
_____
_____
_____
_____
_____
_____

Note: The utility of your current skills should not be abandoned, but accentuated when fusing it with a new idea or tool.

2. Enhancing and expanding your existing skills increases your value and makes you more indispensable in your vocation or business. This practice may be termed cross-training and can lower costs while increasing productivity across a range of areas of life and work in your organization. In 3-5 sentences, discuss the skills that you would benefit from gaining over the next 5 years and their impact on your position in the organization in which you work. (e.g., *Due to our service company expanding internationally, it is prudent for me, as a salesperson, to become more fluent in two additional foreign languages: Spanish and Chinese. Multi-lingual salespersons will be a boon to our organization and an area in which I will expand my skills.*)

_____

_____

_____

_____

_____

_____

_____

_____

Note: Business owners and large organizations are encouraged to utilize a cross-training matrix to cultivate multi-skill mastery for employees. Examples of cross-training tools can be found at: GoLeanSixSigma.com.

3. From your review of learning to give to gain, you know that a prosperous life requires ongoing contributions from you. In 3-5 sentences, describe any areas of life for which you are willing to give and not expect a personal return. This could be community service, charity work, etc. (e.g., *I have joined a local civic club that provides mentoring to underprivileged students. I*

will participate in weekly mentoring sessions with students, and multiple annual events to provide training and exposure to the groups with which I will work. I will also contribute financially to scholarships for eligible students who wish to pursue higher education.)

_____

_____

_____

_____

_____

_____

_____

_____

Chapter III

The Workaholic

• NOTE TO READERS •

The following lecture is presented exactly as it is worded in audio form and retains expressions, terms and references that are applicable to audio only and not common to written communication.

Chapter III

Lecture Title: The Workaholic

Are you ready for your best year yet? Do you want success so bad that you can taste it? If so, this is your time. It only requires you to take three momentous steps in your life and these steps, these seminal moves, force you into greatness. They separate you from the pack. You will no longer be at the lower levels on the totem pole. You will position yourself to first surpass the competition and second outperform any level of achievement you perceived possible.

This is Dr. E.M. Robinson and I want you to fully comprehend what I am about to tell you about your success. To succeed, you must become a workaholic in your area of passion. Let me say that again so there is no confusion. You must become a workaholic in your area of passion. I am sure that you have heard the saying that all work and no play makes Jack a dull boy. But, you should also be aware that all play and no work makes Jack poor. There is no doubt that there is something that you desire to do to reinvent yourself. There is something that drives everyone. If you would relish becoming a renowned dentist with many offices in multiple metropolitan areas, shed stubborn pounds that have plagued you for years or you want to build a family legacy in any domain of business, the following tools will place you not only on your marks, but allow you to be ready and go.

What must be clear is that if you want something in this life, especially something remarkable, something to be envied, you will have to earn it. You must put in work. In the book of Proverbs 12:24, it teaches that if you work hard, you will become a leader; if you are lazy, you will become a slave.[39] I am sure that I have some disbelievers, although this doctrine should bear out in conventional wisdom and logic, but let's investigate this more deeply. You can say to yourself, it doesn't take all that or I wouldn't drive that far, stay in school that long, work all those hours, keep experimenting with that or invest all that money. But, the fact remains that if you're to become that which you desire, you'll have to work and make significant sacrifices. I am not speaking of a little dab will do. I am referring to, in some cases, not months, but years, even decades to bring your ideal to fruition. If you were to ask Tiger Woods how many hours of practice, how many swings, or how many putts it required for him to become a preeminent golfer with the second most PGA tour wins and second most majors, he would most aptly respond, "countless!" I have an adage that I submit to you that will allow you to fully comprehend the notion that to succeed, you must become a workaholic in your area of passion. Here it is: "To truly enjoy the capture, one must be willing to endure the chase." I encourage any high achiever to understand and adopt this maxim as it embodies the mindset required for preeminence. To truly enjoy the capture, one must be willing to endure the chase.

The road to greatness is long, circuitous, bumpy and sometimes dangerous. Yet, the road to preeminence is extremely long, unbelievably circuitous, unbearably bumpy, constantly dangerous and unending. To know great versus preeminent, it is essential to understand that to truly enjoy the capture; one must be willing to endure the chase. This school of thought is best understood by fully internalizing two key concepts. First, is to learn to stop squandering opportunities. Second, is to always exceed the standard. So, if you're truly ready to enjoy the capture, let's become immersed in what the chase will entail.

Learn to Stop Squandering Opportunities

The first idea that is critical to you enjoying the capture is to learn to stop squandering opportunities. It seems if you go from neighborhood to neighborhood in any major city that there are so many people moving and shaking in their communities. From new restaurateurs to civic leaders and activists, there seems to be so much progression. In direct contrast to this advancement, when you venture to certain areas of the city there is great poverty, dilapidation of buildings and wasting away of many lives due to negative behaviors and unending substance abuse.

This diametric difference is the result of capitalization on opportunities versus squandering them. The chasm, put simply, is between gain by using any advantages available to you as opposed to negligence or inaction. When one recognizes the benefits of a position he or she is in and takes steps to reap positive rewards, this allows the haves to continue to have. Ignoring advantages and sitting on one's butt when activity is the solution is why many have nots remain in a cycle of diminishment.

Learning to stop squandering opportunities is the first notion in enjoying the capture. In a recent TED talk, leadership speaker and author, Drew Dudley discussed maximizing potential in earnest.[40] Dudley stated that the scarcity of achievement is not because the ability is not present, but because of squandering talent. This idea is central to understanding the value of taking advantage of doors that are ajar and promotions just a relationship away. This topic is sure to resonate with many minorities because when we view levels of incarceration in the United States, for some ethnic groups, vast numbers of individuals are behind the eight ball. No matter if their mishaps are a function of discrimination or unwise decisions, the result is the same, they have either had their opportunities diminished by outside forces or made decisions that disrupted their immediate chances of success. Further, because so many minorities are taken completely out of the market, they have little to no economic impact. It is one thing to contribute little to society, but it's another to subtract from it. So, stop allowing favorable junctures of circumstances to escape you without acting on them. This is essential to achievement.

Additionally, I urge you to see the value in the

small things that you do each day that can open doors. The small things, in many cases, are the opportunities that should not be squandered. For example, a simple, firm handshake can be the means for being noticed by a potential person of influence or someone who can assist and catapult you toward the perch you aspire to ascend to. Although a handshake is a small action, it's worth is invaluable. It cannot be overrated. It solidifies agreements and relationships. Management experts at the University of Iowa declared handshakes more important than agreeableness, conscientiousness or emotional stability while other studies have shown that the handshake can quickly augment the quality of intimacy and trust in an interaction.[41]

I know numerous individuals who are in ancillary leadership positions that have not taken time to work on their handshake, but I don't know any leaders in what I would consider high ranking positions that have not developed their handshake. I recall a city official in my travels whose handshake was flimsy at best. Whenever I shook his hand, he only used two fingers and his thumb. His grip was not firm, and he barely extended his hand. Consequently, I never felt like he was trustworthy. I was taken aback given his position in the city. I expected him to stand near me leaving about three to four feet between us, extend his right hand, grasp my hand fully, pump my hand two to three times, release my hand and lean back. This never occurred and the agreements made between us never seemed solid.

So, understand that these seemingly small opportunities have value. They can catalyze the reaction of your future. What seems like a routine meeting could be the single most important encounter of your career. What you view as miniscule as it relates to your learning, skills and abilities might be the attribute needed for your movement upward.

Researchers across the board have listed one skill as more important than all others in leadership.[42] Although characteristics such as height and gender dominated in earlier centuries, the single most important skill for leaders in the 21st century is one that cannot be overlooked. This skill allows one to clearly and succinctly explain to their employees any and everything from specific tasks to organizational goals. This one skill is the skill of communication. This is not an area that you can hope will be fine or will improve by default. Deliberately hone this skill. Utilize every opportunity to ameliorate your ability to clearly articulate your thoughts and give clear and adequate direction. This skill is more important than trustworthiness, creativity, timeliness and the like. It aids you in fostering and capitalizing on opportunities when needed. The ability to communicate well is not a skill that you can afford not to have if you are to remain upwardly mobile. This is a skill that when lost due to neglect or the lack of action toward improvement, it serves as a liability as opposed to an asset.

I regularly run into people who say, I should have finished school, or I should have started this business or obtained that certification. I should have been a dentist, or I should have been an attorney. Not squandering the opportunities available to you is a means for eliminating this type of *should have, would have* talk. Don't just talk, DO. Stop hesitating. Get started right now. Work on your goals continuously. When others are resting, having a beer with buddies every weekend or spending frivolously on luxuries, you could be the one who is concentrating on skill improvement, acquiring a certification or building your dream business. It is this small thing, the few hours of reading and studying daily or the research time on skill development that allow you to stand out as opposed to blending into the woodwork. Everyone needs a workaholic in them with respect to some area of passion; and your goals will become a reality when you take advantage of the simple, small, easy opportunities that you have available right now.

To be thorough and clear, it must be acknowledged that there are risks associated with any opportunities. Yet, in the words of Fred Wilcox, you can't steal second base and keep your foot on first.[43] The risk will always be there. So, assess the risk, brace for it and plow through it. And, twenty years later you will not be saying that I should have or would have.

Always Exceed the Standard

We've discussed learning to stop squandering opportunities to an extent that when fully internalized, not even a fool can error. Yet, there is one notion that shouldn't be overlooked, neglected or overrated if you are to truly enjoy the capture of life. This idea is a precept that endures through all recorded time. This seminal teaching is to always exceed the standard. In more vintage terms, it can be conveyed as consistently going the extra mile.

It's best to begin this dive into always exceeding the standard by just thinking about a truly basic concept that can be considered conventional wisdom. This idea is even outlined in biblical scriptures although this lecture is not designed to promote religion of any sort. So here it is: in the ISV version of 2 Thessalonians 3:10, it reads "If anyone doesn't want to work, he shouldn't eat."[44] This is not only simple, but common sense. If you don't work, little will come to you. This is equivalent to the scientific precept of mechanical advantage, or the law of the lever which is: the ratio of the force produced by a machine to the force applied to it. Just as this law is used to assess the performance of a machine, it has a parallel to your personal outcomes. Basically, what you extract from life is proportional to what you give. What you receive is in direct proportion to what you contribute. If you do nothing, expect nothing. You cannot pull out more than you put in. If you put in nothing, you will pull nothing out. So, I encourage anyone who possesses goals that will transform their lives to prioritize work over leisure because to receive, one must give. This is a universal law.

When we peer into this idea in-depth, we see that in the absence of rules, you must possess your own. When lackadaisical mindsets and weak work ethics seem to be the norm, you, alone, must be diligent. When getting tasks done at the last minute seems to be the way, you must be the one who is always prepared well in advance. This allows you to exceed the standard and, in the process, endure the chase. In your vocation or business, it might be common to see neglect of simple things like organization, cleanliness, timeliness or the ability to adjust. This is the juncture when you must consistently take time to know the location of your equipment and supplies, label items of importance, create a system of tracking and always return items to their designated location. This is also when at the end of a shift your team discontinues taking new orders so that the cleaning process begins and it's the closing step for each day. Additionally, this is when the starting time is 8 a.m. the next day, yet your team arranges the tables, seats and decorations the evening before or rehearses multiple times in advance of the big day as opposed to starting at 6:30 a.m. with an hour and a half to spare. Anything can be off kilter and Murphy's Law is always abounding, so why not exceed the standard by addressing every item of business ahead of time? I would be disingenuous if I didn't assert that I have seen both sides and been on both sides. To be clear, I relish the latter more prepared version more so than the helter-skelter, last-minute version.

The master inventor, Thomas Edison, is known for stating that everything comes to him who hustles while he waits.[45] In this precept, Edison is suggesting to us to always exceed the standard. Be proactive; be prepared well in advance. I make this plain because I cling to an adage of my own that illustrates this clearly. Here it is. Those who arrive early can sit where they like; those who arrive late can only stand and watch.

A professional athlete who only practices and prepares himself or herself during the designated training times is fooling themselves if they are intent to outlast their competitors, realize a lucrative contract or ascend to the hall of fame. It is essential that they put in the extra hours before and after practice, condition their body year-round, receive proper treatment for injuries and consume the right balance of nutrients, vitamins and minerals. If they don't, they will be injury prone, playing backup, if at all, or even out of the sport in a hurry. Don't get prepared, stay prepared. In this case, becoming a workaholic in the athlete's area of passion is the signature action that will continuously propel their career.

Just Two Hours

So, how can you expect to receive more from life? It's simple; do more. Stop playing, get real and get busy. Sometimes you must be the circus juggler who keeps all the plates spinning on sticks. Think about it. Just two hours per day can be the impetus to a new, more abundantly inventive you. A single hour in the morning or midday and another before bed can help you establish a new standard for yourself. These two hours daily equates to 14 hours per week. If you consider the 7-9 hours the average person sleeps each day and use the lower limit of 7 hours, this is the point at which the gap between you and the competition becomes grand. With an average day of productivity being 17 hours, just these two hours per day are the equivalent of 728 hours or six weeks per year. This is a month and a half gain. Over a twenty-year period, this is 30 months of production added to your life. This is 2.5 years ahead of your counterparts who are only using fifteen hours daily.

Ostensibly, it's your preference when to use these hours. When you were normally arising at six a.m., you now hop out of bed at 5 a.m. ready to go. This is your method for exceeding the standard. This 60-minute time frame can be your meditative, planning, exercise, preparation for the day, knowledge or skill building time. How it is used is your choice. Just give it a shot.

Personally, when ardently affixed to this regimen, my first hour consists of meditation, hydration activities, exercise, daily list development, and business planning. This approach has yielded positive results for many years. I begin with meditation because it renders me clearly appreciative of life and ensures that I am clearly focused and relaxed. My hydration plan comprises consumption of a specified amount of water and vitamins daily. I do this to promote regularity and foster a strong immune system. With me constantly on the move, this daily dose gives me an advantage physically. My systematic plan of physical activity keeps my body strong and aids in increased stamina and verve. As a matter of fact, exercise keeps the body shapely and attractive which can generate impressive results. The creation of a daily list helps me to prioritize my daily thoughts and actions in alignment with my goals. Some items need to be fresh on the mind to bring them to a conclusion or to allow room for the next order of business to be addressed. And, coordinating business tasks daily keeps me progressing toward my financial goals.

The second hour is usually in the evening an hour before bed. This is my preparation for the next day and business activities time. I contemplate the next day's events, i.e., clothing, food preparation, and organization of my thoughts so that small mishaps don't upend my productivity on the following day. I give attention to multiple business activities, from banking transactions to business product development and promotion.

It's up to you how you utilize these hours, yet I implore you to be attentive to your most definite life goal. This consistent care for your progress will pay large dividends in the long run. These hours allow you to outpace your old self let alone the competition.

There is an old saying that "those at the top of the mountain didn't fall there."[46] This maxim is more than accurate; it's a law of life. If you want to ameliorate your existence, discipline yourself to routinely engage in the activities that improve you, even if it's gradual. These are the actions that the mediocre refuse to commit themselves to. Yet, these are also the behaviors that those who have ascended to greatness have submitted themselves to without ceasing. Further and more important, the people and organizations that have etched their names into the monument of preeminence have these go-the-extra-mile actions embedded in their mode of operation.

Summary

So, let's be clear. Taking advantage of even the smallest opportunities and consistently exceeding the standard will make you an improved version of yourself. But, if you fail to step up, you can expect nothing in return. Simply realize that the floodgates are always open.

This has been Dr. E.M. Robinson with *The Workaholic* and I encourage you to confidently and firmly shake the hand of a potential catalyst to your ascension in your vocation or business, exceed the standard daily by making a habit of going the extra mile. And, you will have endured the journey necessary to enjoy the capture of the greatness or even preeminence that you aspire to. Good day to you.

The Workaholic Reflection & Practice

Instructions:

Answer the following questions honestly and thoroughly and review your responses daily. You are encouraged to copy your responses and post them in a location you will be apt to view each day.

1. Understanding that even small opportunities have value is the impetus for extraordinary success. In three to five sentences, explain, at minimum, two momentous initiatives or projects which you plan to be or are already involved in over the course of the next five years. (*e.g., I recently purchased a vacant lot in a nearby city. The property is coded as commercial and rests along a busy thoroughfare. It will require at least three years to gather the funding for a hotel. I plan to seek out multiple private investors...*).

_____

_____

_____

_____

_____

_____

_____

_____

Note: Capitalizing on the seemingly insignificant opportunities, in many cases, is the beginning of a major, life-altering

undertaking. Be sure to review your response to this exercise monthly to gauge your progress.

Bonus Reflection & Practice
This bonus reflection and practice exercise has been inserted to accentuate the importance of effective communication skills for overachievers.

In seemingly every domain of work or business, the skill of communication must be honed if you are to maximize your potential. On the lines below, honestly discuss the steps you are taking daily to ameliorate your ability to communicate effectively.

_____

_____

_____

_____

_____

_____

_____

_____

Note: Communication is not limited to oral or written forms. Extend your thinking on this activity by considering how you will communicate through body language, dress, temperament, etc.

2. To extract more from life, it is essential to always exceed the standard. Using the lines below, create a list of actions outlining how you will or are prudently using two hours daily; i.e., one hour in the morning and one hour in the evening. Note: If you work a nontraditional schedule, adjust accordingly. (e.g., *Morning: 1.Show gratitude, 2.Meditate, 3.Make journal entries, 4.Make a list of goals, 5.Run 2 miles. Evening: 1.Clean the food truck,*

2.Work in the garden, 3.Prepare foods for the Farmer's Market, 4.Read a prospectus on a technology company...).

Note: This list can be easily adapted to chart form or any work schedule.

Chapter IV

Never Satisfied

Chapter IV

Lecture Title: Never Satisfied

Are you basic, plain, simple, average and just going through the motions? If this is you and you are totally content with this state, stop kidding yourself. You know that happiness is not in being stagnant. It's not found in the same old unproductive routine day after day. Personal satisfaction lies in maximizing your potential. You do realize that you're ready to reach the crest of enjoyment in your life if you begin today reaching for more and extending yourself toward a new you, right?

This is Dr. E.M. Robinson and I would be remiss if I didn't supply you with three tips to end the boredom and discontentment you have with your humdrum routine and feelings of being stuck in park. This lecture is entitled *Never Satisfied*. And, I'm conveying three Cs to keep you pushing the envelope for your improved self. From these Cs, you can bring forward spikes in energy, augmented finances, new knowledge, life-changing ideas and turn a C- existence into an A+ lifestyle. First, is conviction: the strong compelling belief that you will achieve that which you aspire. Second, is commitment. This is your pledge to yourself to ameliorate your condition.   And, third and equally as essential, is collaboration which is you joining forces with allies to extend your reach and productivity to levels that you not only could not have readily conceived in foresight, but also not achieved alone. These three Cs can take you places you have never traveled, refine your knowledge, and push you beyond limits you didn't even know existed. More importantly, these three Cs make a new you. They are simply waiting for you to adopt them, so an explosion of prosperity and positive psyche is at the forefront of your life. So, when you are ready to receive them, the three Cs will appear.

Conviction

The overachiever is grounded in his or her convictions. They must first believe, without a doubt, that they will eventually possess, embrace or experience their goal. This doesn't mean that they won't have fears or setbacks. Stumbling blocks come along with any personal achievement. What transpires in the mind and actions of an overachiever is continuous gravitation toward that high perch on which they would like to rest. They are drawn to their goal as they take each step in that direction. The goal becomes magnetic. If political strategist, analyst, campaign manager, and author, Donna Brazile were prodding the overachiever to move toward their goals, she would likely inform them that "it takes but one person, one moment, one conviction, to start a ripple of change."[47] Author and diplomat, Francis C. Kelly, would be inclined to state to anyone who desires to ascend to preeminence that "convictions are the mainsprings of action, the driving powers of life. And, what a man lives are his convictions."[48]

Professional athletes are pulled toward their goals

daily, through competition, preparation, and intense training. Professional actors and actresses are not outstanding on camera by default. They believe in the outcomes that will result from endless hours of practicing their stage, screen and vocal presence. They constantly hone their abilities to enter another character and engage with an audience. They study without cessation their lines and dramatic techniques. They boost their confidence, energy and creative insight while performing at a level of dedication not common to most.

Conviction is simply seeing in your mind's eye that your goal will come to pass and working toward its end.

One lyric by singer, songwriter, actress, and four-time Grammy Award winner, Pat Benatar, stands out that illustrates conviction inside the psyche of the overachiever.[49] Here it is: "With the power of conviction, there is no sacrifice." This maxim makes conviction as clear as a glass of filtered water. Those who seek to overachieve only surrender to their goal. The long hours, intense study, constant trial and error, decades of experimenting, continuous defeats against a nemesis or years of building are not a loss, but a gain.

Many years ago, I aspired to a Chief Executive Officer position in my field of work. My belief was more than strong, but definite. I began to retain any letters of rejection sent to me by Human Resources Departments when applying for posts of this sort. And, the letters varied, yet they would normally read like this:

Dear Dr. Robinson, (or more informally Dear

Applicant),

Thank you for your interest in the position of Chief Executive Officer (or other position of equal status). We appreciated and enjoyed the opportunity to interview you. At this time, we've decided to proceed with another candidate. Please know that this was an extremely competitive position. We invite you to keep a watchful eye on our job site for any future employment opportunities that may be of interest. We wish you well in your future endeavors.

Kind regards,

Name of Human Resources Director
Name of Institution

I kept numerous hard copies of letters of this ilk. As a matter of fact, I have a book of them. And, this doesn't include the many emails that advised me to "keep applying as there were many qualified applicants, yet we decided to move forward with another candidate whose expertise more closely matches our needs." Numerous letters containing similar language came, yet I continued to insert my name in the hat.

No matter what occurred during panel interviews or phase two or three of the interview processes, I continued to apply. I sharpened every skill. I ensured my credentials were superb, tailored my responses to possible interview questions to the position in question. I improved my presence, articulation, confidence and knowledge of the organizations for which I was interviewing. And, lo and behold, that CEO position came. It was only because of my convictions that this portion of life eventually opened to me.

If you really want to accomplish a goal that in foresight is draining, daunting or would cause the average individual to give up, your convictions will lead the way. What you desire will be reeled closer to you through action, time and a mindset that sees no sacrifice in creating a ripple of change for your life.

Commitment

We have unearthed conviction and particularly how this unadulterated belief is the starting point in great achievements, but we are unfinished without outlining the second of the three Cs buried inside you. To investigate commitment properly, let us first peer into an aphorism that will, without fail, yield clear understanding of your imminent greatness. The aphorism goes like this: For life to be truly fulfilling, it must be a full course existence. I present this precept to you because there is nothing more satisfying in life than the achievement of a large, impressive, lofty goal that not only positively impacts your life, but the lives of many others. For life to be truly fulfilling, it must be a full course existence. This full course existence could be, although not limited to, building a legacy in your domain of business, being elected to a political role that yields unprecedented progressive legislation or becoming a chief executive officer of a corporation whose community outreach yields a new socially responsible corporate image or even patenting an advancement in technology resulting in worldwide adoption and acclaim. So, to digest commitment thoroughly, bear in mind that for life to be truly fulfilling, it must be a full course existence.

Commitment is far from the only "C" incumbent upon you to possess as a distinguishing attribute if you're intent upon bringing forth a new you. An obligation and personal pledge to work endlessly toward your highest achievement is an indispensable characteristic that must become synonymous with you as a being. In few words, commitment materializes as your life's agenda.

A while back, I worked under the tutelage of a supervisor who was revered in my field of work. At one point, after many productive years, he said, "Mr. Robinson, sometimes I can't tell if you're committed. You do your job well and you know your stuff. But, you're constantly working on other things—you're in school studying to obtain another degree, you're running your businesses, and you're involved in all these different things. So, sometimes it just seems like you're not committed." I didn't hesitate to reply. I responded that those things you mentioned: "my dedication to honing my craft, expanding my learning, improving my credentials, and building a financial wall around my family are a testament to my commitment. I'm not sure how I can further show you that I am committed if all that I am doing doesn't." His look in response was a smile and following that conversation, I don't recall him ever questioning my commitment again. I continued to learn more about my vocation, studied indefatigably to increase my credentials all while building businesses outside of my vocation. My commitment to constant advancement in many areas of life was my call to action and I haven't had anyone query me about it since. I am sure that there are those who would say put all your eggs in one basket and keep your eyes on the basket. Commit to one thing to see outstanding results. I don't disagree. Yet, my commitment was more to excellence in all areas of life. This commitment was forged through working to exceed the standard in every endeavor. In my vocation, I routinely arrived early, stayed late and worked to build excellent teams to sustain our successes. In school, I burned the midnight oil studying, organizing my thoughts and sharpening skills relevant to my field. In my businesses, I partnered with my spouse to build our enterprises while still eking out time to consistently show gratitude for life's gifts, be a husband, father, avid cyclist and active member of multiple civic organizations. The results thus far have been positive across many areas of life.

The previous anecdote shows that commitment is a pledge that is unceasingly acted upon. It's a personal obligation. It compels you to act. It powers you through distractions. It allows you to affix your mind and behaviors on a task of interest and see it through. It requires unending movement toward your goals.

If you desire any noteworthy accomplishment to

come into existence, move in that direction and it will gravitate towards you. As you move toward the object of your dreams, it moves toward you.

The direct opposite of this concept is illustrated by the three-toed sloth. This organism is not just sluggish, but essentially idle. It is the slowest mammal on the planet. It is so inactive that algae grow on its furry coat. If you would like to attain a new more exciting and dynamic perch, your mind and body cannot be inert.

True commitment ensures that you're never satisfied with a single win, one championship, or a trophy that sits alone in a large showcase. Commitment plants in your mind the notion that there is much more to accomplish, study, construct, learn thoroughly and refine in your life.

As a teenager, I routinely heard adults in my circle utter a saying that aids in comprehending the true essence of preeminence. The saying is *I went there, and there was no there there.* This colloquialism connotes that a destination is not as good as advertised, a high achievement doesn't satisfy you for long or an endeavor has little meaning once complete. Let's peer into it more deeply. There is a feeling associated with accomplishing a goal. It is the release of dopamine which is a chemical secreted by glands to send signals to parts of the brain and plays a major role in the motivational component of reward-motivated behavior. When you accomplish a big goal, put simply, you feel good. Yet, the second time you accomplish that same goal, the dopamine release is not nearly as satisfying. Only a larger, more impressive goal will sate your desire for achievement. It's only for a short time which leads to even greater feats. Hence, your neurotransmitters need a dopamine fix regularly and even more frequently if you're an overachiever. The big catch leads to the bigger catch as the chemical release is sought again and again to satisfy your psyche.

Your commitment hinges on these dopamine fixes in many ways. A lifetime of accomplishments is not without these great feelings. Nothing exceptional, nothing worthy of complimentary remarks, nothing even remotely outstanding was ever completed without commitment. Legacies are created and sustained through commitment; monuments are constructed to commemorate commitment. When you are committed, the pursuit is endless, leading you to not only surpass your competitors, but to achieve feats that were inconceivable at the outset.

If you disagree, I encourage to see how much you can accomplish without commitment and you can rest assured that you will no longer be a doubting Thomas. Life is not Bewitched or a fairytale in which you can twitch your nose or sprinkle some pixie dust and your dreams are immediately realized. If you want any single, solitary thing of value while on this planet, it requires commitment, and this is a universal law ensuring that you are never satisfied or fulfilled unless your life is a full course existence.

Collaboration

We have unpacked conviction and dissected commitment to see their inner workings. Yet, I would be irresponsible, negligent and unfulfilled if I failed to put forward the third and requisite "C" for anyone who intends to overachieve. This "C" is collaboration and it's the multiplier of all high achievement. It serves as a reagent in the reaction of your preeminence. I frame collaboration in this manner because, alone, the demarcation of your accomplishments can be confined to a time and space. With allies, there are no limits.

Genghis Khan in 1206, didn't become the founder and first Great Khan of the Mongol Empire without collaboration. Khan united numerous nomadic tribes of Northeast Asia and emerged as the largest contiguous empire in history following his death.[50] From Khan, we see that collaboration divides tasks and moves the needle of success to an astronomical degree.

Charles Darwin put forward that in the long history of humankind and animal kind that those organisms that have learned to collaborate and improvise most effectively have prevailed.[51]

There are numerous examples of collaboration generating results that are seemingly out of reach in isolation. An owner of a sole proprietorship can only secure and acquire so many resources. Because they are one, they have limitations. But, the members of a conventional corporation can sell stock engendering vast resources to make significant advancements for the organization. One can only accomplish so much. A group can yield extraordinary results. Individuals on winning teams are credited with victories, but a larger and grander vantage point acknowledges the team. Even Sam Jackson Snead, also known as *Slammin' Sammy*, the holder of the most PGA tour wins, could not have been the first player to win PGA Tour titles in four different decades without the collaboration of his brother, Homer, who showed him how to swing in the back cow pasture.[52]

You did not arrive on this planet without the concatenation of your mother's egg and father's sperm. And, you never won anything without the support of a parent, coach or other team members. This is because collaboration ensures that your results are magnified.

Many years ago, I was appointed to oversee the positive transformation of an organization that, according to the field, failed to meet even minimal standards year after year prior to my arrival. The outcomes were impressive, yet the organization would not have seen such a paradigmatic shift without the development of teams of leaders in multiple areas all working in cohesion.

In the most basic terms, you cannot achieve preeminence alone. The overachiever is not without their supporting cast. If you are to reach your highest levels of productivity, you can never be satisfied with a do-it-yourself-only approach. It requires collaboration, and you will reap the rewards of the strength that comes from work in numbers.

Summary

So, let's make the aforementioned success tools crystal clear. You, the overachiever, must possess the three "Cs" as your linchpin. Conviction keeps you grounded and allows you to move steadily in the direction of your goal. Commitment allows your imminent greatness to emerge as your life becomes a full course existence. And, deliberately collaborating with allies or building teams of leaders augments your achievements.

This has been Dr. E.M. Robinson with *Never Satisfied*; and, these three "Cs" provide you the promise of prodigious accomplishments ensuring that you are never satisfied with a single dopamine fix, but driven to surpass all your previous achievements on your journey to preeminence. Good day to you.

Reflection & Practice Never Satisfied

Instructions:

Answer the following questions honestly and thoroughly and review your responses daily. You are encouraged to copy your responses and post them in a location you will be apt to view each day.

1. Overachievers are grounded in their convictions. Most have mantras or adages to which they subscribe that illustrate their approach to achievement. On the lines below, write or develop three mantras or adages that guide or will guide your notions and behaviors in your ascension to preeminence over the next five years. (*e.g., 1. Today is the only day that is guaranteed. 2. Energy without direction is like a ship without a rudder. 3. Money is a good slave, but a bad master.*)

_____

_____

_____

_____

_____

_____

_____

_____

2. Conviction is the starting point for all great achievements. High performing individuals realize that for life to be truly fulfilling, it must be a full course existence. In three to five sentences, explain any steps that you are taking to live a dynamic life. Include up to 10 areas of life in which you are actively engaged and learning or any fields and activities in which you would

relish being engaged. (*e.g., Learning a second language, restoring antique vehicles and mastering chess are activities that intrigue me. I have purchased an audio foreign language CD for use while driving which I plan to use daily...*)

_____

_____

_____

_____

_____

_____

_____

_____

3. Collaboration is the multiplier of all high achievement. On the lines below, explain a project or initiative and the persons, organizations, etc. with which you will partner to achieve results that you cannot achieve alone. (*e.g., My next venture will require the synergy of Dave Lewis, Malcolm Waits, Joy Turner and me. Our company will distribute condiments and other restaurant supplies throughout the northeast region of the tristate area. Dave will serve as chief of marketing. Malcolm is multi-talented and will manage operations and supply chain dynamics. Joy will be the financial officer. And, I will serve as executive director and oversee the management team.*)

_____

_____

_____

_____

_____

_____

_____

Notes

Preface

1. A. A. Bogomolets, *The Prolongation of life*, (Robinson Foundation, 1946).

2. Board of Governors of the Federal Reserve System, *How many millionaires are there in America?* See: https://dqydj.com/how-many-millionaires-decamillionaire s-america/

3. Escambray English Edition. *Sotomayor celebrates 25th anniversary of his 2.45-meter high jump, See:* http://en.escambray.cu/2018/Sotomay-celebrates-25th-anniversary-of-his-2-45-meter-high-jump/

4. Guiness World Records, *Highest high jump (male)* (Guiness World Records Limited 2019), See: http://www.guinessworldrecords.com/world-records/highest-highjump-(male)

5. Boston Whaler, *285 Conquest*, (Boston Whaler Boats, 2019), See: https://www.bostonwhaler.com/family-overview/conquest-boat-models/285-conquest/

6. The Leading Hotels of the World Ltd, *Laucala Island*, See: https://www.lhw.cowww.m/hotel/Laucala-Island-Laucala-Island-Fiji

7. Tahita.com, *Bora Bora Island*, See: https://www.tahiti.com/island/bora-bora

Crossing the Threshold

8. African American Registry, *Jumping the broom, a short history*, See: https://aaregistry.org/story/jumping-the-broom-a-short-history/

9. O.S. Marden, *He can who thinks he can*, (Kessinger Publishing, LLC 1762).

10. A. Sifferlin, *Time*, See: http://time.com/3398699/confidence-in-the-brain/

11. G. Lubin, *A simple logic question that most Harvard students get wrong*, (Business Insider, 2012), See: https://www.businessinsider.com/question-that-harvard-students-get-wrong-2012-12

12. The Holy Bible, *Matthew 13: 32*, (Christian Arts Publishers, 2013).

13. L. Howes, *Why thinking small is the secret to big success*, (Forbes, July 2012), See: https://www.forbes.com/Forbes/welcom/?toURL=https://www.forbes.com/sites/lewishowes/2012/0706/why-thinking-small-is-the-secret-to-big-success/&refURL=https://www.google.com/&referrer=http://www.google.com/

14. Goodreads, Inc. (2019), See: https://www.goodreads.com/quotes/7969076-each-time-we-face-our-fear-we-gain-strength-courage

15. O.S. Marden, *He can who thinks he can*, (Kessinger Publishing, LLC 1762).

16.   J. R. Flynn, *Asian Americans: Achievement beyond IQ,* (Psychology Press, 1991).

17.   Universe Today, *The life cycle of the sun;* See: https://www.universetoday.com/18847/life-of-the-sun/

18.   K. Broome, *The 8 moon phases in order,* (Science Trends, 2018), See: https://sciencetrends.com/the8-moon-phases-in-order-with-bonus-moon-phase-calendar/

19.   Merriam-Webster, *Webster's third new international dictionary of the English language,* (1993).

20.   CU Connections, *Campus exposure a positive influence on middle school students.* (2014), See: https://connections.cu.edu/stories/campus-exposure-positive-influence-middle-school-students

21.   Aesop, *Aesop's Fables: The grasshopper and the ants,* (Digireads.com, p.86, 2016).

22.   R. Frost, *A servant to servants,* (1914).

23.   Merriam-Webster, *Webster's third new international dictionary of the English language,* (1993).

24.   H. Watts, *The people's tycoon: Henry Ford and the American century,* (Vintage, 2009).

25.   Jesse Yomtov, Full list of every Olympic medal Michael Phelps has won, (USA TODAY Sports, 2016), See: https://www.usatoday.com/story/sports/olympics/rio-2016/2016/08/07/michael-phelps/88361712/

26.   Television Academy, Walt Disney, (2019), See: https://www.emmys.com/bios/walt-disney

27.   R. Umoh, *5 things to know about Robert Johnson, America's first black billionaire*, (CNBC Make It, 2018), See: https://www.cnbc.com/2018/02/26/what-to-know-about-robert-johnson-americas-first-black-billionaire..html

Evolve Your Main Asset

28.   G. Hamel & C. K. Prahalad, *Competing for the future*, (Harvard Business School Press, p. XI, 1994).

29.   M. Beer & N. Nohria, *Breaking the code of change*, (Harvard Business School Press, 2000).

30.   J. Utterback, *Mastering the dynamics of innovation*, (Harvard Business School Press, p. 18, 2nd ed., 1996).

31.   J. A. Angelo, *Choosing curiosity over fear*, (Cornerstone Management Skills, 2019), See: https://www.cornerstonemanagementskills.com/page6

32.   W. Nickels; J. McHugh & S. McHugh, *Understanding business 12th ed.*, (McGraw-Hill Education, 2019).

33.   National Aeronautics and Space Administration, *Newton's third law*, See: https://www.grc.nasa.gov/www/k-12/airplane/newton3.html

34.   G. Fernandez, Importance of family time on kids mental health and adjustment to life, See: https://chil ddevelopmentinfo.com/psychology/importance-of-famil y-time-on-kids-mental-health-and-adjustment-to-life/

35.   W. Nickels; J. McHugh & S. McHugh, *Understanding business 12th ed.*, (McGraw-Hill Education, 2019).

36.   Aesop, *Aesop's Fables: The grasshopper and the ants*, (Digireads.com, 2016).

37.   R. E. Riggio. *There's magic in your smile*, (Psychology Today, 2012) neurotransmitters. See: http s://www.psychologytoday.com/us/blog/cutting-edge-leadership/201206/there-s-magic-in-your-smile

38.   S. Maital, *Executive economics: Ten essential tools for managers*, (Free Press, 2011).

39.   The Holy Bible, *Proverbs 12:14*, (Christian Arts Publishers, 2013).

40.   D. Dudley, *Everyday leadership*, See: https://www.y outube.com/watch?v=_Ay6EawKKME

41.   The Muse, *Why your handshake matters (and how to get it right)*, (2019). See: https://www.themuse.com /advice/why-your-handshake-matters-and-how-to-get-it-right

42. M. Bondurant, *The importance of communication skills [Top 10 studies]*, (Inlp Center, n.d.), See: https://inlpce nter.org/importance-of-communication-skills/

43. Bleeding Espresso, *You can't steal second with your foot on first*, See: http://bleedingespresso.com/2011/08/ you-cant-steal-second-base-with-your-foot-on-first.html

44. The Holy Bible, *2 Thessalonians 3:10*, (Christian Arts Publishers, 2013).

45. V. McClelland, *Wise words and quotes*, (Tyndale House Publishers, p.4, 1998).

46. V. Lombardi, *Vince Lombardi quotes (Move Me Quotes, 2019)*, See: https://www.movemequotes.com/ta g/vince-lombardi-quotes/

Never Satisfied

47. D. Brazile, *Quotes ray*, (QuotesRay.com, 2017), See: https://www.quotesray.com/quote/it-takes-but-one-per son-one-moment-one-conviction-to-start-a-ripple-of-cha nge

48. F. C. Kelly, Conviction sayings, (Wiseoldsayings.com, 2019), See: http://www.wiseolds wayings.com/conviction-quotes/

49.   P. Benatar, *Invincible*, (PatBenatarVEVO, 2009), See: https://www.google.c om/search?client=firefox-b-1-d&q=pat+benatar+invincible

50.   History, *Genghis Khan*, (A & E Television Networks, LLC, 2019), See: https://www.history.com/topics/china/genghis-khan

51.   C. Darwin, *On the origin of species*, (Digireads.com., 2016).

52.   D. Anderson, Sam Snead, *Smooth-swinger winner of record 81 PGA tour events, dies at 89* (The New York Times, 2002) See: https://www.nytimes.com/2002/05/24/sports/sam-snead-smooth-swinging-winner-of-record-81-pga-tour-events-dies-at-89.html

EPILOGUE

The preceding chapters offer readers four lectures containing tools, advice, tips, research, observations, incidents, anecdotes and the like as a means for constructing an enviable lifetime of accomplishments.

Chapter I conveys the means for overwhelming and defeating any nemesis you face. Making a decision and launching your plan immediately, increasing your self-confidence, using your time wisely and pursuing your obsession unrelentingly are deemed as four keys to crossing the threshold. Making a decision and launching your plan immediately allows you to take the plunge into your new life instantly. Increasing your self-confidence gives you an unwavering belief in your ability to bring your most compelling goals to fruition. Prudent use of your time engenders heightened productivity daily. And, an unceasing pursuit of your obsession makes your ascension imminent.

In Chapter II, extending your existing skills and augmenting your marketability are put forward as means for creating a personal evolution. Combining the old with the new, enhancing your skill set and giving to gain are offered as characteristics essential to becoming an overachiever. Combining the old with the new simplifies your evolution as you transform into a more advanced version of yourself. Enhancing your existing skills increases your value to yourself and others. And, giving to gain leverages you as not just a recipient of the rewards of life, but a provider.

Chapter III throws a strong light on stepping up when opportunities present themselves as the method for reaping an outstanding return on life's investment. Not squandering opportunities and always exceeding the standard are the practices that ensure you make the most of the hand you are dealt. Learning to stop squandering opportunities helps you view even the smallest advantages from the proper perspective. And, always exceeding the standard is a principle that opens the floodgates of excellence in your life. These success tools help you to endure the journey and enjoy the capture of greatness in your life.

In Chapter IV, three linchpins of success are presented. Conviction, commitment and collaboration are elucidated as the tools that allow you to surpass any previous level of achievement. Conviction keeps you gravitating toward your goals. Commitment makes your life a full course existence as you improve daily. And, collaboration provides you the catalyst for extraordinary achievements that would be unreachable alone.

In sum, the notions presented in this collection of lectures are indispensable points of wisdom for anyone seeking above average outcomes for their life. I encourage all persons who will not relent until their ultimate goal is realized to study this text in-depth, subscribe to its precepts and share with their family and friends.

Bonus Lecture I:

Strike a Nerve

Bonus Lecture I

Lecture Title: Strike a Nerve

Have you gotten off the couch yet? When you had your last big idea, that life-changing plan, you were sitting on the couch. You can sit there if you like, but if you want to make those social improvements or accomplish those business and physique goals, you must get off that couch.

This is Dr. E.M. Robinson and I am obligated to no longer sugar coat things for you. If you want to bring those goals to pass, get off that couch. I know that it strikes a nerve for you to hear that you've been lazy, you haven't given your best, you left too early, you quit too soon, or you let yourself get tired, but, I am sure this is the only means for getting you off that couch. No one else is going to move your limbs for you. It's up to you and you only. If you are serious about achieving that dream, you must get off that couch.

So, I have three pieces of advice that are sure to spur you to action while you are still sitting there. First, is to understand that little things mean a lot. Second, is to realize that your goal is easy if you have a guide. And third, over time you will learn to love the work that leads to accomplishment of your goals. If these three points of advice don't convince you, let me express this in a fashion that is as clear as a glass of pure filtered water. If you keep sitting on that couch, you will end up old, unaccomplished and only a shell of what you could have become. So, now that that we've struck a nerve, let's dive in so you can get some activity in those limbs.

Little Things Mean a Lot

The first notion of utmost importance when considering accomplishment, especially if you have been consistently delaying action, is to understand that little things mean a lot. Earlier in this lecture you were implored to remove yourself from that couch as the first step. This might seem small, but it's the beginning of the journey toward your dreams. You cannot run a marathon without the first step. Of course, significant training is key, yet the first step can send you into the thicket of the journey. Without the initial step, you remain static, stuck in a rut and stagnant.

What I would like you to consider is that a single shot can bring down a large beast. When David triumphed Goliath, it was not because of an army of weapons.[53] If you're familiar with this account, David kept his father's sheep. In doing so, he had rescued sheep from the mouth of the lion and bear—seizing them by the hair, striking and killing them. Likewise, when facing Goliath, David took a stone from his bag and using his sling, slung a stone into the forehead of Goliath. The stone sank into Goliath's forehead and he fell face down on the ground. This triumph was due to David's faith that his God would carry him through. And, it remains obvious that a simple stone and sling brought down the giant. So, first understand that little things mean a lot and this can be the small breakthrough you need in your life to create a sea of prosperity.

Even honey bees, in their diminutive state, can unleash more than just pain. [54] Their most important defense mechanism, a sharp, barbed micro-syringe about ¼ to ½ inch in size can pierce the skin injecting apitoxin, a potent venom. For someone with a bee sting allergy, just one sting might have them in the emergency room or even cause death.

It was not because Ray Kroc was endowed with extensive retail innovations that he became the fast-food king, but because of one idea emanating from him joining the McDonald's brothers in the 1950s.[55]

In just a few words, one idea can spur the transformation of an industry. A single spark can trigger an explosion.

Further than that, the Pareto Principle also known as the 80/20 rule or the law of the vital few puts forward that, for many events, roughly 80% of the effects come from 20% of the causes.[56]

Little things mean a lot. When I was thirteen, my grandfather and father trained me the basics in the cemetery monument industry. They began by teaching me the installation process, which is the final step in satisfying a client. This small beginning led to me develop comprehensive understanding and outstanding ability in this industry including detailed knowledge of inventory, sales, pricing, stenciling, sandblasting, delivery and site construction. Just this simple start was the impetus for my acquisition of a wealth of skills in the field of monument production.

A classic example of little things mean a lot comes from the life of Malcolm X.[57] Malcolm X taught himself to read and write in prison through use of the dictionary: copying page by page, struggling to enunciate the terms and committing the definitions to memory. Study of this one book, the dictionary, was a starting point for a leader of remarkable repute of the 1960s and his personal means for transforming from a hustler to a disciple.

A newly constructed, fishless pond can become highly populated with fish over time by the simple actions of eggs or fry being carried in on the feet or mouths of waterfowl or other animals. Eggs can be affixed to aquatic plants added to the pond or flooding can wash fish from nearby ponds, lakes and streams into the pond.[58] The result can be a vast of array of fish types and other organisms over time.

Even a single female housefly can reproduce 5-6 times laying up to 150 eggs per batch.[59] At that rate, the existence of this insect is seemingly never in danger.

One business idea can launch you into prosperity over time. You just have to get off that couch.

Thomas Edison's light bulb is still burning because he decided to try a carbonized cotton thread filament.[60] This small adjustment translated into world change.

I urge you to discover inside you that one, simple thing that you can do to get started on the path to your ultimate desires. This whisper can be the reason for your explosion as a person. When you understand that little things mean a lot, not only will you get off that couch, but you will be taking the first step in your marathon of life. From this tiny beginning or simplistic idea, you will have established the birthplace of your personal transformation.

Success is Easy if you Have a Guide

The second piece of advice that I offer to spur you to action is a commonsensical notion. Since many do just enough to make a living or limit themselves because of fear, doubt and procrastination, it is incumbent upon the overachiever to know unequivocally that it can be easy to succeed if you have a guide. Underpinning this guide, I urge you to keep it simple.

You do not have to swing for the fences every time you're at the plate. Yes, you are prodded to think big; yet, sometimes a routine single can lead to numerous runs.

Keeping it simple makes the difficult easy. By creating an easy-to-understand step-by-step plan to achieve a goal, this can be your breakthrough. When making this plan, you think the task through and account for many of the circumstances that are likely to result as you progress. Creating this detailed plan is not just proactive, but the means for overcoming obstacles that are sure to emerge. What is key to know is that a solid plan makes each future action step obvious as you progress. The plan is your recipe. Follow the recipe to the letter and the dish will turn out properly. Take small steps, do one thing at a time and don't overreach.

When learning to play tennis, you first must know

the rules of the game of course, but initially to clear the net with your serve or return ball to make the game interesting. So, just focusing on the simple tasks of serving to the proper point, your ball's clearance of the net and landing in bounds can provide you enjoyment of this sport even as a novice.

A few years back, I was tasked with completing a five-chapter dissertation. My first few attempts included writing using a lengthy outline and submitting two chapters at a time for review. After a significant struggle using this approach, I had a mentor instruct me on how to complete the document not, chapter by chapter, page by page, paragraph by paragraph or even sentence by sentence, but word by word. This method, once I developed the skill, allowed me to complete sentence by sentence, paragraph by paragraph, page by page and chapter by chapter with ease and speed toward swift completion of the entire literary project. Keeping it simple reduced the complexity of this undertaking and allowed me to finish much more quickly.

If you are climbing a ladder, each rung must be stepped on in your ascent so that you have stability along the way. It is prudent, if not essential, to refrain from skipping steps or move in haste lest you fall. In school, life, business and relationships, this is a universal law. Keeping it simple makes the difficult easy.

The value simplicity can be astronomical. If you research some of the most successful people in our country, they kept it simple. Sam Walton focused on volume sales and low prices to build the largest retail system of stores in the world. This was done through buying in large quantities directly from manufacturers and selling vast amounts of items at a low markup for greater total profit.[61] The Coca-Cola Corporation created the largest beverage company in the world through focuses on brilliant marketing and relentless salesmanship.[62] These organizations kept it simple. They focused on one craft, a non-complex method or a user-friendly business model en-route to a fortune. If you can sell enough soap, you don't have to sell water. If you can sell enough water, it could be distraction to sell soap.

A key concept that many fail to acknowledge is that if you live in the United States, a capitalism-centric, free enterprise system, the windows of opportunity are gaping and seemingly never close. Even if one does close, without delay another one opens. The U.S. economy is robust and a single, simple idea can permit you to tap into abundance and return gifts to you that you could not have been readily conceived in foresight.

Thus, I posit that you keep it simple since a nerve has been struck to encourage you to add kindling to that fire in your belly towards completion of your goals.

Learn to Love the Work That Leads to Accomplishment of Your Goals

The third and final item that I will evoke to strike a nerve with you is that over time you will learn to love the work that leads to accomplishment of your goals. In life, we all take actions that bring great joy once we experience success or achieve some level of mastery. In this regard, I ask that you add the following adage to your repertory of sayings and repeat this as often as possible. The adage is: if you improve your skill, you will increase your enjoyment.

If you improve your skill, you will increase your enjoyment makes sense on all fronts as you experience euphoria when you perform at a high level at any task.

For example, perfecting your favorite dish involves tweaking the recipe, learning what ingredients give your dish appeal, honing the dish's presentation and repeating the process. This work can bring on a salvo of accolades from partakers and a surge of happiness comes as a result of mastering the dish.

The Orthodontist

The notion if you improve your skill, you will increase your enjoyment spans seemingly all skills and acquired talents. Consider the work of an orthodontist in-depth.[63] Following attainment of an undergraduate degree, completion of dental school and a postgraduate orthodontics program, earning a board certification and becoming licensed, an orthodontist experiences delight because of the improvement and increase in her skills. She is also bestowed ongoing enjoyment from her work once she has begun to practice. She evaluates a patient's teeth to determine the severity of the bad bite: whether it's an overbite, underbite, cross bite, or overcrowding of teeth. She engages in the critical planning stage in which a study model is created through castings and bite impressions. She takes panoramic X-rays to see the exact position of teeth and each root. She then creates computer generated images and compiles the before treatment photographs. From there, she takes the patient through the active stage in which a custom, fixed or movable orthodontic appliance is used to gently move the teeth into proper alignment. Frequent office visits are scheduled to allow the orthodontist to regularly adjust the device to ensure adequate and continual pressure is being applied to the teeth. During treatment, photographs are also taken to show progression. Upon completion of the treatment, the orthodontist removes the appliance and creates a custom fit retainer for the patient and takes the after-treatment photographs to show the improvements that have been made. The orthodontist engages in this practice continuously throughout her career. And, as her quality of treatment advances, the number of satisfied patients and enjoyment for her practice grows. When you improve your skill, you increase your enjoyment.

In every field of work and every task, there is a sequence of learning that occurs. You move from novice, competence, proficiency and expertise to mastery.[64] Once you arrive at the higher levels of skill: proficiency, expertise and mastery, the enjoyment from the time, energy and work that you must contribute leads to bliss. You will not consider the numerous steps, practice, study, organization, preparation or travel involved in your task to be drudgery; it becomes pleasurable to your psyche.

I urge you to find an area of learning or work on an activity for which you have at least a passive interest and begin to develop your knowledge and skills. You will find that the more you know about the topic and the more you engage in its relevant work, the more you will glow when speaking on this subject.

Several years ago, I recall taking a pair of expensive shoes to a shoe repair shop for a heel replacement. Upon entry, I began to engage the owner concerning the process of repair. I casually asked him how he got into the business and what he liked best about his work. I was amazed by the length of his response and the passion with which he spoke concerning shoe repair. His face lit up, he smiled and talked with his hands. I could not get a word in edgewise. Not only did he speak endlessly about shoe types and repairs, but his conversation focused heavily on what most people don't understand about the skill and expertise necessary to produce a quality product. The shoe repair man showed that when you improve your skill, you increase your enjoyment.

This seems to go without saying, but it must be stated and fully comprehended that as you move towards preeminence in your area of work improving your skill increases your enjoyment.

My family doctor is an avid cyclist. I am a cyclist. If I bring up cycling during an office visit, I not only receive the best treatment, but engage in a lengthy conversation mostly led by my physician. This is because he has put a tremendous amount time into developing his cycling knowledge and it shows in his smile and eagerness to share his cycling experiences even with other patients waiting.

So, improve your skill in your area of passion; and, you will experience an endless euphoria on your quest to increasingly higher levels of achievement.

Summary

We have dissected little things mean a lot, success is easy if you have a guide and learning to love the work that leads to accomplishment of your goals. As a recap, I encourage you to never neglect to immerse yourself in an activity that you can continuously learn more about and ameliorate your skills. If it is your business or businesses, a hobby or even a special dish, the more you improve your skill, the more you will increase your enjoyment.

This has been Dr. E.M. Robinson with *Strike a Nerve*. So, please know that your journey of transforming into that maximum version of yourself does not end with understanding that little things mean a lot, success is easy if you have a guide and you will learn to love the work that leads to accomplishment of your goals as you improve your abilities. Your transformation is ongoing. You will see that a single idea can bring forth a wave of benefits and rewards, keeping it simple can be the spark that allows your prosperity to explode and increased skill increases your pleasure. So, now that a nerve has been struck, I am sure that you will hurriedly get off that couch and take that first step that allows all your desires to be within your quick and easy grasp. Good day to you.

Bonus Lecture I: Strike A Nerve

NOTES

53. The Holy Bible, *1 Samuel 17: 1-58*, (Christian Arts Publishers, 2013).

54. Science Daily, *Bee sting.* See: https://www.science daily.com/terms/bee_sting.htm

55. Money, *The founder and the complicated true story behind the founding of McDonald's,* (Money, 2018), See: http://money.com/money/4602541/the-founder-mcdo nalds-movie-accuracy/

56. K. Kruse, The 80/20 rule and how it can change your life, (Forbes, 2019), See: https://www.forbes.com/ sites/kevinkruse/2016/03/07/80-20-rule/#4a4c22b83 814

57. The New York Times, *When X=Literacy,* (1993), See: https://www.nytimes.com/1993/01/06/opinion/ when-x=literacy.html?mtrref=www.google.com&gwh= A54B04BA7782AE67E2B2A3082F208D61&gwt=pay

58. ScienceABC, *Where do fish come from in new lakes and ponds?* (ScienceABC, 2019), See: https://www.scienceab c.com/nature/animals/where-do-fish-come-from-in-new -lakes-and-ponds.html

59.   Reference, What is the life cycle of a house fly? (Reference, 2019), See: https://www.reference.com/pets-animals/life-cycle-house-fly-eff3302239255926

60.   The Franklin Institute, Edison's lightbulb, (The Franklin Institute, 2018), https://www.fi.edu/history-resources/edisons-lightbulb

61.   S. Walton, Sam Walton: *Made in America.* (Bantam, 1993).

62.   F. Allen, *Secret formula: How brilliant marketing and relentless salesmanship made Coca-Cola the best-known product in the world*, (HarperCollins, 1994).

63.   Erickson Orthodontics, Inc. *Steps of treatment.* (Erickson Orthodontics, Inc. 2019), See: http://www.menifeebraces.com/steps-of-treatment

64.   S. E. Dreyfus. The five-stage model of adult skill acquisition, (Bulletin of Science Technology & Society, 2004), See: http://www.bumc.bu.edu/facedev-medicine/files/2012/03/Dreyfus-skill-level.pdf

Bonus Lecture II:

Stop Keeping up With the Joneses

• NOTE •

Each lecture in this text is presented exactly as it is worded in audio form and retains expressions, terms and references that are applicable to audio only and not common to written communication.

DISCLAIMER:

The following lecture provides information that the author believes to be prudent concerning the subject matter it covers, but is sold or rendered with the understanding that neither the author nor the publisher are proffering individualized advice tailored to any person's needs. A licensed professional should be sought if one needs expert investment, legal or accounting assistance.

BONUS CHAPTER

Lecture Title: Stop Keeping up With the Joneses

Are you still keeping up with your neighbors and friends? They get a timeshare, so you get duped into buying one and only use it twice in four years--pay the maintenance on it while numerous others use and pay for the same piece of property and use it only twice in four years. Sound familiar?

Or, for show, your friends buy a luxury vehicle that they really can't afford. They struggle dearly to make payments on it and place a ton of purchases on their credit cards just to keep up this appearance. And, then you go out to a dealership, like a dum-dum, and sign on for 72 months at a high interest rate. If this is you, and you don't ever want to become wealthy then continue. Be my guest. But, if you desire to accumulate a fortune, stop! Stop right now! Stop keeping up with the Joneses.

This is Dr. E.M. Robinson and I am supplying you with some fundamental financial acumen and personal development success tools to help you start operating in the black even if you've been in the red for years. It's never too late to learn some of the proven strategies of the wealthy. So, if you're like many millions of Americans living paycheck to paycheck or can't survive without your job more than a month, listen up. We will keep this very simple so it's easy to understand, to get started and remain on the proper trajectory toward prosperity. We'll discuss five proven-to-work strategies that will allow you take back your finances or, at minimum, steer them in the right direction. So, let's digest these tools.

Now, to ensure that you're not running neck and neck with the Joneses anymore, I encourage you to first let your imagination be your guide. Second, become a sponge so you will have the skills to compete for the future. Third, learn to master little money to achieve big results. Fourth, stop trying to be all things to all people. Lastly, is to view your success as exclusive to you.

These five notions and actions allow you to achieve in this world, but in your own realm. You won't be keeping up with the Joneses; you will be the Joneses.

Let Your Imagination be Your Guide

I would like to start by tackling letting your imagination be your guide. Many people that I have conversations with, no matter the venue, whether its conferences, seminars, or presentations in my field of work, seem to think that all valuable innovations are already used up. That is simply not the case.
There is a universal law that all things change over time. Out with the old, in with the new is not just an adage, but it is a law of the universe.

In this age of ubiquitous technology and vast advancement, we are no longer in the technology age, but what has been deemed by many as the psychozoic age.[1] This is the age of the mind, when whatever you conceive can be brought into existence.

Back in 2007, having worked with small and medium-size businesses all over the U.S. and Canada, I had a short stint in which I was out of work. Letting my imagination be my guide, I created a plan of consulting to offer services well beyond what I'd supplied when I was a company employee. I expanded my business model to include employee training, employee manual construction amongst other additions and saw in six months my client base triple, bringing me twice the income I was making working as an employee. Albeit, it was short-lived, my imagination put me immediately back in the game catapulting me to my next business endeavor without a financial let down.

Gary Hamel and C.K. Prahalad's intriguing work, *Competing for the Future,* it is clear that imagination is essential to advancement.[2] These instructors of innovation make it plain that to compete for the future, combining the old with the new is the way. This is critical. It's equivalent to being part of the establishment while being a member of the movement—like the pager to a text message alert or the 1995 Camry to the 2019 Prius. Basically, the combination of the old and the new is the means for constant ingenuity and remaining relevant.

For some innovations, it's the fusion of quality and durability with ease of use. Or, quite possibly, taking the old model of a bottle holding apparatus, extending the number of bottles it can hold and adding a swivel and lift-release mechanism.

Imagination is central to getting out of that rut and

129

allows you to not compete with the Joneses, but be the Joneses. I earnestly encourage you to employ your imagination. Let it be your guide. Don't dismiss your imagination; it can be the difference between basic and advanced. When the ideas flow, write them down. Capture them for future use. Make them real by putting massive action behind them. Get started by, at least, placing them on your schedule for action later. Just putting your ideas in writing can be the smidgeon of motivation needed to continue toward the completion of goals that you couldn't readily fathom coming to pass beforehand. Strike the hammer while the iron is hot. When the brain is working, capitalize on it. When you conceive that clairvoyant plan, take it on. Pursue it and you can escape keeping up with the Joneses. Why be part of the pack, when you can be the leader of it?

In 2007, Warren Bennis and Burt Nanus wrote in *Leaders: Strategies for Taking Charge* that a healthy structure can be possessed only when it has a clear sense of what it is and what is to do.[3] It is another way of saying, choose a direction and stick with it. If your direction is financial independence, focus and act on it. Don't make that unnecessary purchase. Don't buy big to look rich. Don't keep up with the Joneses. Employ your imagination.

If you are, for example, skilled in creating fantastic barbecue cuisine, providing golf or yoga lessons, why not make this your niche? Why not take your ideas and skills in any area of expertise and turn them into a money maker?

When you have that burgeoning idea, go ahead and execute. This will separate you from the crowd and over time with appropriate study, skill honing, proper pricing, the right place, apt promotion and constant improvement of your product, you will see the financial and self-improvement advantages that you are creating for yourself.

Unleashing your creativity can be the difference between you and the crowd. So, don't hesitate to let your imagination run free and be your impetus for an improved you. This is the foremost way to avoid keeping up with the Joneses.

Become a Sponge

The second characteristic that I implore you to develop is to become a sponge. To compete now and in the future, you must continuously learn and develop new, relevant and useful skills. There are skills that we all possess at varying degrees and levels, but could vastly improve with a little study, time and effort. These are excellent opportunities for capitalizing on what we already have. Learning more about that current skill, whether it's sewing, finance, carpentry or an endless list of other crafts, could yield astronomical results. In your current vocation, it could be as simple as spending a little time obtaining an apt certification or training to acquire a new skill. Note that if you're already endowed with ability in an area and you have an affinity for the craft, becoming immersed in study will not be drudgery; it will be fun.

Becoming a sponge involves interest, passion and experience over time. To be that person that absorbs things thoroughly and becomes furnished with seemingly esoteric knowledge on a subject, there are three actions that I suggest.

Read Incessantly

First, is reading. Reading is essential. Read everything relevant to your goals; create balance between fiction and non-fiction. According to bestselling author, speaker and media contributor, Tom Corley, it takes the average self-made millionaire 32 years to become rich. And, individuals who achieve this status have the habit of reading for self-improvement daily.[4] Corley also states that more than 85% of those millionaires read more than two books per month. Warren Buffett has been quoted as saying that he read between 600 and 1000 pages per day at the start of his investing career and continually devotes about 80% of his day to reading.[5]

The result of learning and refinement of knowledge that comes from this level of information absorption is not only to one's boon for ameliorating their existence, but is the catalyst for becoming extraordinary. Not only does this type of ongoing study aid in changing your thought pattern and perceptions, it bodes well for adjusting your behavior to meet any of your goals. So, the surefire way to become a sponge is to read incessantly.

Investigate Topics In-depth

The second means for becoming a sponge is investigating topics in-depth. When acquiring new vocabulary, you not only need to know the definition of the term, but you must gather comprehensive and useful knowledge about the term. This could include spelling, pronunciation, how it's inflected especially when the term changes parts of speech, any additional grammatical information about the term, how the term collocates or what words are usually used with it and the context in which the term is most likely used.

An executive chef is required to master culinary arts to a level of depth that is usually surprising to the novice cook. A physician, likewise, possesses a superb knowledge in their area of specialty. To be clear, developing thorough knowledge of topics is the second most effective means for becoming a sponge.

Apply Reading and In-depth Study

The third and most obvious means for becoming a sponge is application of what one learns through reading and in-depth study. If you are reading a large volume of helpful literature, it makes sense to put your learning into practice. Even when learning vocabulary, there is a tendency to lose the readiness to utilize the terms that you've learned if you haven't given utterance to those terms regularly. It's very simple. You understand and absorb any topic better when you apply your learning.

American educator, Edgar Dale, developed the cone of experience in the mid to late 1900s. Dale theorized that learners retain more information by simulating the real experience more so than what they hear, read or see.[6] Applying what you learn is the basis for retaining what you learn. This process ensures that you become a sponge.

During my youth, one of my mentors clung to a simplistic, but befitting adage when referring to learning. This mentor would invariably state: "the only way to learn is by doing." This mentor worked indefatigably applying new learning in culinary arts and horticulture. Each time I visited this mentor, there were some new things to share: a unique creation in the kitchen, a dish that was seasoned to perfection or an obscure plant that had been cultivated.

So, becoming a sponge involves endless reading, in-depth study and applying new knowledge. This is the second step in breaking the cycle of you keeping pace with the Joneses. When you are a sponge, you're the pacesetter and others will be keeping up with you.

Master Little Money for big Results

The third method I urge you to employ to stop keeping up with the Joneses is one that just cannot be neglected. It is learning to master a little money for big results. If you can't handle small responsibilities, how can you expect to manage larger ones?

Your income is likely one of your greatest

assets. Yet, to reach that new peak, you should take steps to ensure that you retain an increasingly greater portion of your income and receive a greater return on the money you invest. Thus, you are encouraged to develop proficiency in the use of your earnings to continuously make gains. English philosopher, statesman, scientist, jurist, orator, and author, Sir Francis Bacon, is known for the adage: money is a good servant, but a bad master.[7] For many people, money serves them well for their current needs, yet can be the means for their financial demise with respect to their wants. Mastery of money can be an arduous task when you already have bad habits. If you constantly expend more than you earn shopping for unnecessary trinkets or designer items or spend excessively on entertainment and dining out, these practices can keep you operating in the red. So, kicking some these habits is critical to financial independence.

In *Action Redoubled Volume II*, we talked at length about simplistic ways to gain control of your finances. The first area that pundits point to as it relates to saving money is to limit dining out. Overindulgence of this convenience, for many, is the reason for their lack of solvency or ability to build wealth. Planning and preparing your own meals aid in cutting costs and serve as the first line of defense against insolvency. It allows you to instantly reduce your expenditures, although at first glance, routinely dining out might seem nominal.

Put simply, attention to the outgo of controllable expenses is the central piece to mastering little money for big results.

Danko and Stanley, the world-renowned researchers and authors of the bestseller, *The Millionaire Next Door*, outlined two key concepts that should be your guide to mastering little money for big results.[8a] From their longitudinal study of millionaires, they found that most millionaires became that way not because of how much money they made. Their financial success came by way of: I) budgeting and controlling expenses and II) even upon achieving millionaire status, they did not deviate from frugality, which allowed them to remain affluent. Danko and Stanley's investigation led them to state that "it is easier to purchase products that denote superiority than to actually be superior in economic achievement."[8b] Essentially, Danko and Stanley throw a strong light on the notion that the bulk of millionaires are not spendthrifts. They became financially well off and remain that way because they are frugal.

Note, this aspect of not keeping up with the Joneses is easier said than done. Once you gain mastery in this area, you will find that it is a matter of mindset and changing your habits.

More than a decade ago, my wife and I began setting aside 10% of our income after participating in a free financial management course. It was explained to us, much to our delight, that financial independence is not about how much you earn, but what you retain and the investments you make that bring a return. After making this slight change, we began to see our savings mount and we were more easily able to invest in businesses that brought us impressive returns. Over time, our spending habits changed completely. We focused on bargains or deep discounts when purchasing seemingly every item. We ensured that our purchases were of high quality, but only bought them when they were on sale. We limited our dining out, prepared more of our meals and continuously invested in endeavors that brought a return.

Our case is also one of a little at a time produces outstanding results. Saving a small amount each pay period, preferably 10% or more, will build a nest egg over time. As well, investing a small amount in the right ventures over time will make you a fortune. What we learned unequivocally was that, over time, even a slow drip will fill a large bucket.

So, I implore you to master small money for huge results; this allows you to avoid keeping up with the Joneses as you become superior in economic achievement as opposed to material possessions.

Stop Trying to be all Things to all People

The penultimate precept I offer to shield you from just being a member of the pack is to stop trying to be all things to all people. You can't satisfy everyone. You can only satisfy yourself and this, in itself, is a daunting task.

Be you and only you. If you are spending time copying your friends and neighbors, you are not spending time improving you. Even in Romans 14:5, it states, "Let every man be fully persuaded in his own mind."[9] This is wise counsel and even more prudent when practiced. It is excellent to have friends; it is also gratifying to have certain material possessions. Yet, I urge you to exercise your own sage judgement when considering expensive or unaffordable purchases just to fit in or be held in high esteem by others. If acquisition of a status symbol inhibits your financial stability, I advise you to avoid making that purchase until it is not a hindrance to your finances. Just because it is popular to possess an expensive product should not be your goad to the action of purchasing it, especially if it creates a financial setback. Necessity should fill this space first. Materialism can be a deadly financial disease. It is easily remedied by you being persuaded by your own mind and sagacious management of your income.

In terms that are not sugarcoated, stop trying to be all things to all people. They get a boat; you get a boat. They think you should drive a more luxurious vehicle because it's apparent that you have the income to afford the purchase; you make the expensive upgrade. They take cruises three times per year; you break your personal bank to go with them.

Only you know your financial circumstances and only you can control them. So, I speak in earnest when I say to stop keeping up with the Joneses requires you to focus on satisfying you and not copying the behaviors of friends or having the same ideals as your neighbors. Following their minds as opposed to your own might have you in foreclosure, dreading going to the mailbox or struggling dearly to make ends meet—when all you had to do was be persuaded by your own mind.

Your Success is Exclusive to you

The fifth and final piece of advice that I offer to you to preclude you from being stride for stride with the Joneses is that you must learn that your success is exclusive to you. I believe that this notion requires repeating. You must learn that your success is exclusive to you. I am sure that you realize that your failure is exclusive to you, so why wouldn't your success be exclusive to you?

There is an English proverb that states that every man's neighbor is his looking glass.[10] And, there is also an adage that an unusual amount of common sense is called wisdom.[11] You cannot, in simple terms, focus on comparing yourself to others if you desire to ameliorate your own existence. Common sense informs you that if you focus anywhere other than yourself then out of necessity you are not focusing on you.

You are you and no one else. What others are doing is their project. If they succeed, it's fine. It's their business. To be frank, what's it to you? When you travel to work, your timeframe is irrelevant to all other drivers. When you graduate from an institution of higher learning, your degree is conferred to you only and bears only your name. If you receive a promotion; it's yours alone. And, the direct opposite of each of these outcomes is exclusive to you as well.

The 25-page Paper

I recall a story from my travels that I like to call the 25-page paper that illustrates the point that your success is exclusive to you. When I was working on my MBA in the early 2000s, I was taking the capstone, also known as the final course, for the program. This class required each student to be placed in a group of four and collaborate to construct a 25-page paper on some topic in business.

After being assigned to a group, we began to discuss our plans to complete the paper through email exchanges. Having a solid background in writing and editing, I explained to the group that if each group member (including myself) provided me with six pages of material with references seven days before the deadline, I would put it all together. This meant making each group member's material cohere in to one, editing the paper for grammar and typos, meeting all other writing style specifications and submitting the finished product to the professor. One group member objected to this approach stating that I really wasn't going to be doing much because the paper would be pretty much finished when I received everyone's work. Yet, I retorted by explaining that I would be doing more work than any other group member due to the umpteen hours involved in editing the paper. So, we all agreed to this method and I awaited their submissions of six pages with references.

About five days before the paper was due, not a single group member supplied me with any information and I was becoming concerned. I emailed the group members to extract their portion, but it came in slowly.

Three days before the deadline, I was perplexed having only received 11 pages of material from my group members. My concern was warranted considering that the requirement was 25 pages. I emailed the group again to have them send more information, but nothing came. Under any other circumstances, especially early in the program, I would have been livid and possibly reached out to the professor to explain the lack of cooperation of my group members. Time was running short. I spent the next couple of days researching material in abundance to make up for the deficit of information received from the other group members. I made what I received from the group cohere, added the additional pages of information necessary to meet the 25-page requirement, edited the paper, quite crisply I might add, and submitted the paper on time.

I copied the group on the submission email and thought to myself, I couldn't worry about the other members of the group; I wanted an "A" in the course. I received a reply to the copied email from one of the group members informing me that the paper looked great. I simply responded "thanks" as I wanted nothing else to do with this group. I was resolved to believe that it didn't matter what grade the other group members received, I was only concerned about my grade.

A day later, the professor sent me an email stating that my group received an "A" on the paper. The professor also explained that the students in my group were fortunate to have me in the group. And, that she wished me continued success in my career.

My only concern was my grade and my degree. I took no thought for the grade that the other group members made. My success was exclusive to me even as the other group members were beneficiaries of my labor.

From the story of the 25-page paper, it is as clear as a glass of tap water that your success is exclusive to you. Learn this concept thoroughly so you can avoid being simply one of the multitude.

Summary

Overall, we have discussed five essentials you must readily conceive and master in earnest to stop keeping up with the Joneses. Letting your imagination be your guide ensures you tap into your uniqueness separating you from the crowd. Becoming a sponge encompasses endless reading, in-depth study of topics and readily applying what you learn permitting you to continuously compete for the future. Mastering little money gives you the foundation to handle large sums with prudence. Learning to stop trying to be all things to all people, cements you as original. And, knowing that your success is exclusive to you enables you to gear your thinking around a laser-like focus for completion of your goals.

This has been Dr. E.M. Robinson with *Stop Keeping Up with the Joneses.* Subscribe to these five principles and you will be allowing your imagination, sponge mindset, mastery of finances, originality and self-focus to be the slow drip that fills your large bucket of knowledge and wealth over time. And, you won't be chasing the Joneses, you will be the Joneses. Good day to you.

Bonus Lecture II: Stop Keeping up With the Joneses

NOTES

1.   B. Tracy, *Psychcozoic age*, See: https://yourfavortie milk.wordPress.com/2014/09/12/psychozoic-age

2.   G. Hamel & C. K. Prahalad, *Competing for the future* (Harvard Business School Press 1994).

3.   W. Bennis & B. Nanus, *Leaders: Strategies for taking charge* (HarperCollins Publishers 2007).

4.   T. Corley, *In 5 years of studying rich people, I found self-made millionaires have 7 habits that help them build wealth* (Business Insider September 2017); See: htttp:// www.businessinsider.com/self-made-millionaires-habits -build-wealth-2017-9

5.   A. Merle, *The reading habits of ultra-successful people* (Wellness, December 2017), See: https://www.h uffingtonpost.com/_Andrew-merle/the-reading-habits-of-ult_b_988130.html

6.   H. M. Anderson, *Dale's cone of experience*, See: http: //www.queensu.ca/teachingandlearning/modules/activ e/documents/Dales_Cone_of_Experience_summary.pdf

7.   Goodreads.com, *Francis Bacon quote* (Goodreads.com, 2019), See: https://www.goodreads.co m/quotes/446478-money-is-a-great-servant-but-a-bad-master

8a.   T. J. Stanley & W. D. Danko, *The millionaire next door* (Pocket 1996).

8b.   T. J. Stanley & W. D. Danko, *The millionaire next door* (Pocket 1996), pp. 28.

9.   The Holy Bible, Romans 14: (Christian Arts Publishers, 2013).

10.   V. McClellan, *Wise words and quotes* (Tindale House Publishers, Inc. 1998), pp. 182.

11.   V. McClellan, *Wise words and quotes* (Tindale House Publishers, Inc. 1998), pp. 47.

CLOSING THOUGHTS

Today, the notion of personal success is at the forefront of the minds of many people. In fact, thoughts about achieving one's ideal version of themselves is more than a trend. It is the driving force in the lives of throngs of individuals. This primary impetus for accomplishment is personal satisfaction—the sense of fulfillment from having wants or desires satisfied. For some, personal satisfaction is the one life goal that must be realized over time as it results in the emergence of a more complete crystallized version of the individual.

The tools provided in each chapter of this text are the second tier of fundamentals in the structure of that which is necessary to move from considerably above average to one's highest levels of achievement. To be clear, this book aptly follows the footing and slab introduced in *From Great to Preeminent: Success Tools for Overachievers Volume I.* In that text, eliminating doubt, redoubling your actions to augment your productivity, excellence in contemporary leadership through employing the 3 "Ps" and refraining from keeping up with your neighbors and friends are outlined. And, from the principles put forward in this second volume, the structure of your greatness will begin to take shape. This shaping can be likened to the framing of an edifice of your choosing.

For some, crossing thresholds and enduring the chase of their ideal renders them visibly different from what they once were. The time and effort that underpins this transformation become a fixation and the large goals that are being pursued become closer in proximity.

At this juncture in your pursuit, having embodied the precepts in the first iteration in this series of books, your previous best in an area of work is now mediocre and the acme of your ability is a continuously moving target. The lessons in this second volume are now the conscious motivator helping you to forge ahead through continuously capitalizing on your time and effort.

If you have pursued eliminating your employer, you now possess the tools to do so. And, you know and understand unequivocally that the journey will not be easy, yet you are determined and savvy enough to plow through any circumstances you will encounter on this path. If you have decided to move vertically in your vocation, the instruments of change are now embedded in your psyche and deportment to the extent that you cannot be relegated to a role beneath your newly acquired skill set. If building a conglomerate in business has been your goad to action, the breadth of your mind's evolution is now such that this goal is within your easy reach.

To be clear, you are at a momentous point in your development. The chasm between the extant you and the old you widens each day. You have stretched. You only seek to move to new levels of excellence as daily improvement has become your habit. You are now residing in the realm of great as preeminence beckons. As your summit self calls out, you recognize the apparent magnitude of your personal possibilities.

Due to the intellectual tools you have acquired and

the deportment to which you have subscribed, you realize that preeminence is only achieved when you do more. Thus, fear, doubt, and procrastination are constantly kept at bay as you move closer to the head of the pack of the greats. You constantly cross thresholds, deliberately develop your mind, work indefatigably and are never satisfied with even your highest achievements. Your best continues to be deemed as mediocre and you will not relent until you have surpassed all levels of achievement that you conceived possible.

As a final statement to catapult you to exceed your zenith in your area of passion, I leave you with this:

Whatever you have chosen as your greatest concentration will also be your greatest attribute.

Good day to you.

The Author

E. M. Robinson is a veteran educator, serial entrepreneur, author and lecturer. Robinson is the current president of Robinson Enterprises-MS, LLC, overseeing retail and real estate operations while serving as an administrator in Shelby County Schools and Adjunct faculty in the Educational Leadership Department for the American College of Education. Robinson also served as Adjunct faculty in the Business and Legal Studies Division of Southwest Tennessee Community College. Robinson is the former Superintendent of Schools for Durant Public School District, magnet school director, principal, and assistant principal for Clarksdale Municipal School District and teacher of the sciences in multiple high schools and middle schools in Mississippi. He holds a B.S.E. from Mississippi Valley State University, M.A. from the University of Mississippi, M.B.A. from Regis University and Ph.D. from Mississippi State University.

Contact

Mississippi Office:
Dr. E.M. Robinson & Associates, LLC
1169 S. Dr. Martin Luther King, Jr. Blvd Suite 4
Grenada, MS 38901
Email: edwinmarcusr@gmail.com

Tennessee Office:
Dr. E.M. Robinson & Associates, LLC
1095 Links View Ln W
Cordova, TN 38018
Email: edwinmarcusr@gmail.com

Enjoy lecture excerpts at our YouTube Channel:

https://www.youtube.com/channel/UCzBMZDkIhB-3K5-Pbg1IO6Q

Find more books by E.M. Robinson at: Amazon.com, Google Books, Barnes & Noble, Kindle and other outlets.

For information about availability for speaking engagements, book signings and presentations, please logon to:

https://docs.google.com/forms/d/e/1FAIpQLSdl4a03YemPK8cj z3TTV9OlOD5MBto9O2XuDqz3ePDZwHyECA/viewform?c=0 &w=1

Other Books and Lectures by E. M. Robinson, PhD

Books

From Great to Preeminent: Success Tools for Overachievers Vol. I.

Rudiments of Existential and Antithetical Existential Logic (2018);

Analysis of Clarksdale Municipal School District's Eight Magnet Schools in Relation to Accountability Status and Student Expenditures (2016)

Coming Soon

The Jump: A Success Manual for all High School Graduates (Spring 2022); Teach Like a Pro: Essential Skills for Master Teachers (Fall 2022); The Can Philosophy (Spring, 2023)

www.ingramcontent.com/pod-product-compliance
Lightning Source LLC
Chambersburg PA
CBHW021417210526
45463CB00001B/414